DREAM ON...
NOW DELIVER

The no nonsense guide to achieving
success in the entertainment industry

PATRICIA
KARA

Published January 2024
ISBN paperback: 979-8-9891962-3-4
ISBN Hardcover: 979-8-9891962-4-1
Library of Congress Control Number: 2023924012
For information address:
The Three Tomatoes Book Publishing
6 Soundview Rd.
Glen Cove, NY 11542
Cover design: NYCArtDirector.com
Interior design: NYCArtDirector.com
Cover photo and author photo: Sofia Spentzas-Tranchitella

PRAISE FOR
DREAM ON...NOW DELIVER

"Through her perseverance and caring attitude, Patricia has been able to navigate and succeed in the entertainment industry without losing her humanity."

~ Michael A. Alfieri, Founder/Producer, Miantri Films

"I just wish I had this book when I was first starting out as it would have saved me a lot of time and confusion."

~Sarati: Actress, *Deal or No Deal*, Case #12

"Patricia has been thriving in this industry for a long time...the book is warm, genuine, honest and full of exceptional advice...I wish I had known these things when I started out."

~ Elena Evangelo, Actress, Filmmaker, Director

"Dream On...Now Deliver is an invaluable bible for anyone who wants to make it in the entertainment industry."

~ Larry Kasanoff, Producer, Writer, Author

"With this book, Patricia is imparting her hard-earned wisdom to help anyone looking to not just break in, but stay in the entertainment industry."

~Summer Bellessa, Model and Actor,
Deal or No Deal Case Model #25

"Through this book, Patricia has paid it forward, helping young people, actors, actresses, models and giving them the advice to help them be better at what they do and be successful for years to come!"

~Lou Maggio, Former Director of Photography
for Venus Swimwear, Film Producer

"I can't think of a better resource for somebody to help you succeed in the entertainment business than Patricia. She has tapped into all aspects of the entertainment industry and knows how to build a business for the long term."

~Dave Sinclair Host (on-camera and radio) and Actor

Dream On...Now Deliver will teach readers how to organically hone their craft, network within the business and ultimately find their place in the industry."

~Deb Mellman, Publicist

"This book is filled with invaluable insights, common sense approaches to challenges, inspiring stories and real-world advice detailing how to become successful while taking chance out of the occasion."

~James Rendek- Founder/Chief Creative Officer,
One Partners Advertising

*Dedicated to the memory of my mother,
Eleftheria Konstantaki, whose strength was,
and will always be, the ultimate example.*

Dream On ... Now Deliver

DON'T QUIT

When things go wrong, as they sometimes will,
When the road you're trudging seems all uphill,
When the funds are low, and the debts are high
And you want to smile but you have to sigh,
When care is pressing you down a bit
Rest if you must—but don't you quit!

Life is queer with its twists and turns,
As everyone of us sometimes learns,
And many a failure turns about,
When he might have won had he stuck it out;
Don't give up though the pace seems slow,
You may succeed with another blow.

Success is failure turned inside out,
The silver tint of the clouds of doubt,
And when you never can tell how close you are,
It may be near when it seems so far;
So stick to the fight when you're hardest hit,
It's when things seem worse, that you must not quit.

~ by Edgar A. Guest

Dear Reader,

I wrote this book to be a practical guide for anyone who wants to build a successful career in the entertainment industry. I had to learn and find my way when I started, and I really only had my instincts and the phone book to help me figure it out. My sincerest hope is that this book serves as an instructional resource and a source of positive encouragement whenever you are in the dark or start doubting yourself.

Everyone needs some supporting people in their lives to cheer loudly through the successes and the failures, so if you are still looking for those people, let this book and my words be among your loudest cheerleaders! If you combine the right amount of hard work and some luck, you will make a lot of good decisions, build a network of good people to help, and you will overcome every tough break on your way to another big achievement!

I have had too many ups and downs to remember them all, and you will see that the entertainment industry is largely about working through disappointments and what feels like failures. In those moments, you will have to engage your inner-most strength and find a way to believe in yourself more than anyone else and push forward. You will need to have the ability to turn to yourself when there is no one else there to lift you up.

Years ago, when I was living in New York City, I remember leaving an audition and stopping to browse a nearby outdoor flea market. I was new in the city, still figuring everything out in one of the biggest and most competitive cities in the world. Even though there were so many people around me, I was far away from everyone who knew me, and I felt alone.

As I browsed the various art and wares, trying not to dwell on how my audition might turn out for me, a framed poem caught my eye. As I stood there, I realized that I had read the words written by Edgar A. Guest several times without a single distraction preventing me from absorbing the poem fully. I snapped back into the moment and bought it immediately. I went straight to my apartment and placed it next to my bed so that I could read these words every day forward.

I still have this framed near my bedside, and yes, I still read this poem every day.

Now it is up to you to decide what you want to accomplish and how you want to accomplish it in this crazy world of entertainment. You will be tested, you will fail, but if you find what you have inside you to keep pushing forward, you will also succeed, and you will learn how to advance and keep earning what you want from your career. When you struggle to find motivation, let your competition motivate you, knowing that someone else out there is fighting along with you to be the best they can be; let your peers in the business be your competition AND drive. Eventually, you will find your rhythm, your mantra, and you will do it every day as you climb your own personal ladder to the top.

Paraphrasing Mr. Guest, no matter what, be committed to trying again, because one more try may be all it takes to achieve everything!

Patricia Kara

CONTENTS

FOREWORD

In the landscape of the entertainment industry, where dreams are chased and aspirations are nurtured, there are those who possess a true understanding of the inner workings and the hidden secrets that pave a path to success. These people possess a wealth of knowledge and experience, and their insights are invaluable. In this book, Patricia has opened the lock box.

When we think about the entertainment industry, we often envision the glitz and the glamour, the bright lights, and the allure of fame. It's an industry that captivates our imaginations and draws us in with its larger-than-life personalities and extraordinary talents. But behind-the-scenes lies a lot of hard work, determination, and countless stories of perseverance.

In Patricia Kara's book, *Dream On…Now Deliver*, she shares the truths, insights, and invaluable lessons she has learned throughout her journey. As a beloved model on the iconic series, *Deal or No Deal*, Patricia has experienced the highs and lows that come with pursuing a career in entertainment.

This book is not just a mere collection of tips and tricks, it's Patricia's personal guide, her roadmap for aspiring entertainers who are looking to make their mark. It's the book she wishes she had when she was 16 trying to find her way into the business. She shares the wisdom she has gained, providing invaluable insights into the industry.

From navigating auditions, casting calls, understanding what it means to need and obtain an agent, and the importance of creating a personal brand with a lasting impact and social media presence. Patricia offers her practical advice that is grounded in her own lived experiences. She emphasizes the importance of hard work, resilience, and continuous self-improvement, reminding us that success is not handed to us, but earned through dedication and determination.

What sets this book apart is Patricia's genuine desire to uplift others and share her knowledge. She understands the power of mentorship, the impact of guidance and the importance of paying it forward. Patricia's generosity shines through as she offers a helping hand to those who are embarking on their own journey breaking into the entertainment business.

Dream On...Now Deliver is not just a guidebook for aspiring entertainers; it is a testament to the human spirit, to the power of dreams, and to the belief that with hard work and the right mindset and commitment, anything is possible. Patricia's personal story serves as a reminder that behind the glitz and glamour lies a world of dedication, drive, and unwavering passion.

I am honored to write this foreword and to commend Patricia Kara for sharing her insights and experiences. This book will empower and guide those who read it, encouraging them to chase their dreams and make their own mark. May you find inspiration and direction to pursue your dreams, just as Patricia has done.

~Mashawn Nix, Emmy winning executive producer and television executive.

INTRODUCTION

Congratulations—you are taking steps toward a career in front of the camera. Perhaps you are young and setting out on your own, or maybe you have years of experience in some other field and want to make a career change. You may have been in the entertainment field for a little while, and you're looking for a new approach. Wherever you are, whoever you are, no matter your age or experience, there is a place for everyone in the vast, global entertainment industry. Think of all the faces you've seen on all the screens your entire life. All those people who have appeared on your favorite shows, the commercials in between segments, the billboard at your local intersection—every single one of those people started where you are.

You may have tried to talk yourself out of it—or in a more likely scenario, someone in your life has. The industry has many naysayers who talk about broken dreams and high rates of disappointment and failure. Perhaps that's true if your definition of success rides on being super rich and famous. While you might attain that elite level of success someday, I'm not here to tell you how to do that.

As you read on, you'll notice how often I say *you are a business.* Your pursuit of working in the entertainment industry counts as dedication to building a career and a livelihood: it's neither a hobby nor a pipedream.

I'm going to help prepare you for the entertainment industry and teach you how to consider yourself a business within it. Becoming a successful business? That starts with how you decide to define your success.

When I started in the industry over 30 years ago, I had no connections, no money, and no internet access. I had the Yellow Pages. That's right, *the Yellow Pages*. Mine was a long process of trial and error. You will, similarly, be thrown into new and foreign situations that will require you to adapt and use your instincts. You may be new to this business, but you'll still have an instantaneous response to a decision you're facing before all the over-thinking kicks in. Instincts develop with experience, and, over time, you will learn to trust them. And though I will give you guidelines to help you prepare for uncertainty, experience will be your best teacher, and good instincts will become a very helpful resource. This is true everywhere, but it's especially relevant in the entertainment industry.

- First and foremost, you will learn how to look at yourself as a business.
- You will learn all the various players in show business by their industry names—manager, agent, and more.
- You will know which photos to use for headshots, as well as when and how to use them.
- You will learn that an audition begins before you've even entered a room of casting directors.
- You will learn how to turn rejection into a resource.
- You will learn that the job doesn't stop when the camera stops rolling.
- You will learn that every introduction you make counts—and how to make it count.
- And yes, we will discuss how social media has entered the game.

ONE

SMALL JOBS

By taking even the smallest jobs in front of a camera—or, if not a camera, the public eye—you are removing yourself from your comfort zone and cracking open a door to the vast, foreign world of entertainment.

When I started out in the business, I was in my hometown of Chicago, hungry for any kind of work in the field. I applied to *everything*: extra/background roles in television and film, modeling jobs in local commercials and trade shows, and just about anything else entertainment-industry-adjacent.

To find jobs like these, check out local theater websites for gig and audition notices, Backstage.com, social media outlets, theater workshops, university film departments, and anything else that crosses your path. There are many local Facebook groups and Instagram accounts that post casting calls—you are likely to discover such groups via word of mouth and by following relevant threads and hashtags.

Think of these small jobs as the first few sentences on your résumé. We will talk a lot more about résumé-building later, but for now, remember that as you seek small jobs, there is always a casting director, **agent**, or client involved in the hiring process. These are the people who decide if you can play the part before you even audition, and your job will always be to tell them that you can. This fact never changes—no matter how big or small the stage.

When I was starting out, I didn't understand my own versatility yet. I went after jobs that I thought were a close fit. I couldn't see yet, for example, that I had the ability to play the "girl next door"—but much to my surprise, one of my early jobs was for a hair ad that sought that "type." You'll naturally want to limit yourself in the beginning, so it will benefit you to break this habit early. Instead, think of the tangible skills you have. Do you know how to play tennis? Good—put that on your résumé. Are you a good bullshitter? Call those "improvisational skills." Do you identify with a specific heritage? Promote that. It all matters. Those little quirks, skills, and facts about you are all assets. Please don't lie or embellish your skills, however—you will likely be asked to display them.

Perhaps the most important lesson from these small jobs is how to work with others in the industry. This will be your first introduction to all the different players. Treat everyone you meet as shareholders of your business: with respect. The people you meet in the business are not your steppingstones—they are individuals on their own path. That extra you worked with for a few days might someday become a producer. I have worked with fellow actors who became agents and assistants who became film writers. A little respect goes a long way, and while not everyone you meet will necessarily remember you, they will if you were unpleasant. You've heard about being canceled? It happens regularly in the biz.

Now, that's not to say you can't strive to get ahead and stand out—you'll still need to differentiate yourself from your competitors. It's just unfortunate that so many people take this to mean that you must steamroll over everyone else. So: what does it mean to stand out? It means being interesting and having a few fun skills and quirks in your back pocket, yes. But it mostly means that you are a pro at introducing yourself, being inquisitive, and projecting a positive attitude.

LEARNING

As you seek and book these small jobs, you will inevitably learn something new. You will see what goes into a production, and you'll discover the types of roles you like and dislike. There is much to be learned, even if you're playing a small part. This exposure is necessary—but it won't necessarily teach you talent and skill. Even if you have a natural talent for the performing arts, I recommend seeking out classes, workshops, and coaches. Even if you are the most talented person in your town, you will face tougher competition as you advance in the business, so it's going to benefit you to hone your skills and get into the habit of learning and improving.

You may see postings for such workshops and coaches in the same places you look for small jobs. Most of them have social media accounts where you can learn more about the course structure and available programs. Oftentimes, the workshops are tied to a theater and have a particular area of focus, like Shakespearean drama or comedy; you may have heard of the Second City, which is a famous comedy theater in Chicago—and where many well-known actors and comedians learned their craft via **improv** classes. Many of the instructors will allow you to audit (try) the class before you decide to make the commitment—they may even allow you to partake in a scene or exercise.

Small jobs, alongside these acting classes and workshops,

will make you more comfortable with performing. If you've never performed in front of a crowd or camera before, the idea can be very intimidating. The nerves you have early in your career are the same ones you'll have during your big break—they never go away. Don't let your nerves talk you out of the business. This is all part of your conditioning: you must constantly work your body's muscles for them to work properly, and the same goes for your performance "muscle." By conditioning that muscle, your performances will improve and become more natural. Being a real person who can make your nerves work for you adds a layer of connection and vulnerability to your work.

The cost for professional instruction varies by city, the popularity of the class or workshop, and the number of sessions. If you are working with a small budget, start by watching television and film with a focused lens. Pay attention to the actors you like and notice how they connect with their characters. Notice how they move, their tempo, their facial expressions. Watch different kinds of shows—you might discover that your interest as a consumer isn't the same as your interest as a professional. Maybe even watch some commercials and game shows while you're at it, especially if you're interested in appearing in them.

When I started out, people told me that I needed to choose one department: film, television, or modeling. That advice no longer applies to today's culture, as there is more overlap between departments than ever. High-profile film stars are booking **indie** films and television series. Comedy actors are taking game show hosting jobs. Television-series regulars star in commercials for cool clients. Don't worry about picking and sticking—just pay attention to what interests you most. Another key tip: start recording yourself acting as much as possible. This learning period will come in handy for your reel (more on reels later).

For those of you who are primarily interested in modeling, look at print ads for homework. Create a Pinterest board for online content or go old-school and buy some magazines. Start saving the print ads you like and analyze your connection to what you've saved. For instance, is it the model's makeup that catches your attention, or perhaps the way they are posing or conveying a certain attitude? How is the model representing the brand?

Once you've conducted your analysis, here's an assignment: pick a brand you like, pretend you've just been booked for a job modeling their new collection, and style yourself, posing in front of the mirror. How would you approach this job? You can take it a step further and have a friend take styled, posed photos of you. Post the photos on Instagram and poll your followers. Which are their favorites, and how else do they respond? Tag the designers or stores where you purchased the clothing and accessories or the salon that keeps you groomed. You can also reach out to other small businesses, as local boutiques and salons are always looking for models! You may not be paid, but you'll probably get a trade for clothes or products, so you'll benefit in the end from the experience and reward. Just to reiterate, this should all be included on your résumé.

CHECKPOINT:

- Find and apply for small jobs in your city.
- Make a list of your quirks, skills, and strengths.
- Network with locals working in the entertainment industry.
- Get into student mode and sign up for classes or coaching.
- Watch actors and hosts in a wide variety of genres and ask yourself why you like their work.
- Study print work you like. Practice styling yourself and posing in front of the mirror and/or camera.

TWO

ALL ABOUT AGENTS

Your next assignment is to narrow down a list of agencies. This is also your first test.

When you begin this assignment, you'll discover that there are so many different agencies that represent various niches and mediums: there are agencies for print ad models; swimsuit models; fit models; **voice-over** actors; social media **influencers**; youth, senior, and runway models; and more. This is a test because it will challenge you to expand any preconceived images you hold of yourself in your head. When I started out, I thought certain jobs were "not me" or "long shots," but agents or casting directors had different ideas. The part of our brain that talks us out of something is often just self-doubting noise. **Keep this in mind: don't limit yourself and don't listen when others limit you but do listen with both ears when they see something more in you.**

As you narrow down your list of agencies, you should start thinking simultaneously about the kind of work that interests you. By now, you should know that my advice is to be as open-minded as possible during this process. Next, start looking up agencies in your home city. Agencies in smaller-market cities (i.e., any major city that is not New York City or Los Angeles) may not have work in all the specific categories; however, there's an advantage to working with smaller-market agencies for a new actor. It's a way to start working without taking the enormous risk of moving, while still booking gigs to fill in your portfolio or reel. Remember: *If you want to be in the entertainment business, be in the entertainment business. Take the work that comes your way.* Seek out what's closest to you, even if you are in a smaller-market region.

If you're starting this process with a large social media following, I would recommend reaching out to agencies with established influencer departments. Clients are paying big bucks to represent their brands via social media, and this could be lucrative for the influencers among you—just keep in mind that influencer agents typically look for influencers who have 100,000 or more followers.

Once you have developed a list of agencies, start researching them to narrow down your list. I want to take this opportunity to bust a myth. Many people think you can only have one agent. We see this echoed in popular culture: the term "call my agent" comes to mind from television and movies. This belief is generally untrue, however, especially when you are just starting out. It is perfectly acceptable to reach out to different agents in different categories: one for modeling and one for television, for example. You may run into a situation where an agent wants you to be exclusive—that's fine, but make sure that you do your due diligence and research all the options before signing with just one. We call this kind of agent-talent relationship **across-the-board**, where one agent is representing you across multiple categories.

Boutique vs. big: a quick word about agency size. Some smaller agencies will tell you, "We already have someone with your look in this category," while other agencies—typically the larger ones—won't care how many clients they have in a single category. But there's a downside to going big: it's much easier to get lost in the shuffle of a larger agency. The boutique agencies are more likely to remember you and give you extra attention.

SUBMISSIONS

Once you've narrowed down your list of agencies, it's time to research each one individually. You must look not only at their website, but their social media presence as well—particularly Instagram. Your aim should be to learn their submission process, familiarize yourself with the agents who work there and determine the kinds of talent they gravitate toward. Take lots of notes and stay organized. It's easy to lose track.

There are many agencies, more than ever before. I'm old-school and like to write by hand and keep a physical schedule book, but others may prefer using a digital device of choice. You'll want to use the same means of keeping notes later in the process to track the people you meet and what they said. Keep this habit: even when you think business is booming, don't forget to take notes.

You'll notice that some agencies will allow you to submit online while others have **open calls**. Open calls are informal invitations to meet with an agent during a certain time frame. The open calls are typically posted on the agency's website. Sometimes the open calls posted online will get specific about the type of talent they want down to height and measurements. Don't get too hung up on these requirements. I once saw an open call for models 5'8 and up and showed up with my 5'6 self and a pair of heels and ended up signing with that agency.

Agents who hold open calls will usually be upfront and tell you then and there if you're a good fit for them. Take this opportunity to learn and make an impression. Agents will most likely ask you questions about yourself, so prepare something interesting to tell them. Bring a résumé and photos. If they are acting-specific agents, they will ask you for your reel. If you are meeting with a modeling-specific agent, be prepared for them to take a photo of you on the spot—I will elaborate on this later, but unless otherwise noted: style yourself in natural hair and makeup, and dress in **nice casual wear**. In other words, look presentable and fashion-forward, but not formal or dressed in business attire.

If you have the opportunity to meet face-to-face, this is always the better option—but if your only option is to submit online, do so. Not all agencies will use the words "submit" or "submissions." Look out for keywords like "Get Discovered," "New Talent," or "**New Faces**." You may encounter ads that look like they're from legitimate agencies because they use the same language, just be wary of scams and never enter payment or sensitive information if prompted.

Some of the agencies—usually the larger ones—are word-of-mouth only. You can easily identify these: they will be the ones with nothing but a "Contact Us" page on their website.

REFERRALS

Remember when I mentioned that some agents will tell you when you're not a good fit? They may offer to refer you to a different agency. If they do refer you, make sure to always give credit where credit is due. Mention the person who referred you. You'll remember them because you wrote it down, right?

It always helps to keep your ears open. You'll start noticing the agent topic come up in everyday conversation with friends and colleagues. "Who's your agent?" is a question you'll hear *a lot* in places like L.A. or New York. You'll start noticing specific agents' names everywhere, in fact. You'll get to know them in this informal way. For instance, there's usually a sign-in sheet at in-person auditions where you must write down both your name and your agent's name, and I would take a minute to look at the names on the list to get a sense of who's who. There are more popular agents and less-known ones, but the only thing that matters is if they are a good agent for *you*.

CHOOSING

You've done the research; you've made the submissions; you've heard from a couple of agents. Maybe you're faced with a choice of who to work with. Maybe you've been invited to just one meeting. One meeting is an opportunity, even if it's with an agent who may not have been at the top of your list. If they are open to working with you, take the time to listen to their feedback and let them go to work for you. You have nothing to lose.

As you meet with the prospective agents, especially if you haven't done this part before, you'll learn a lot. They will tell you which roles they've encountered lately and which they envision for you. You may learn about roles you've never even heard of before. At this point, as you still learn about the business, your job is to use your instincts.

Pay attention to how you feel about what the prospective agent is telling you. Even if you're not super interested in the kinds of roles they envision for you, stay open-minded. And if what an agent suggests makes you feel uncomfortable, trust your instincts there as well (e.g., if they suggest a role that makes you uncomfortable or compromises your ethics).

So, what makes a good agent? In the beginning, and always, you'll want someone who will work for you. That means submitting you and pitching you to clients. In short, they're good if they're working actively to get you the auditions. If you are a business, your agent is your sales rep. They don't get paid until your talents are sold. Your job is knowing your value.

Even though your agent will require you to be adaptable and open-minded about roles, you must still remember that you are a business with a lot to offer. In the beginning, you will be excited to get any opportunity, and that's a good attitude to have—but don't forget to voice what you are or aren't comfortable doing (for example, a beef commercial if you are a vegetarian or a role that requires nudity if you feel that request crosses a personal boundary).

As with any career, you will level up with time and experience. I see "entry-level" roles posted regularly, but I am more selective now that I've established a personal standard (for the job itself, for the pay, etc.) that's aligned with my years of experience. Trust that you will get there, and make sure to have conversations about your value and your boundaries with your agents.

A good agent, just like a good talent, will understand that the key is working together as a team. This is a relationship not unlike the other relationships in your life: it will require hard work on both sides, mutual respect, and communication.

Do you remember when I mentioned that some of you may get only one meeting? Take the meeting and work with the agent, but if the agent ends up being less than team-minded, learn all you can from the experience and keep searching for the right one.

That brings me to my final point about the agent-talent relationship. There may come a time when you must leave your agent for another. Again, like any relationship—there may come a time when you've outgrown it. You'll usually sense this first instinctually. Just like in a personal relationship, both talent and agent must do equal shares of the work.

Just like in a personal relationship, if one or both of you is slacking and doesn't make efforts to be better, the relationship is headed for divorce. You may be tempted to stick it out because you'll remember all the good times: the amazing roles you booked together and the times the agent went to bat for you. Don't forget that you have a lot of value to offer. Muster up the courage to make the decision that's right for you.

I once had a great agent who worked hard for me for a long time, but over time, it became clear that we were growing apart. I was no longer getting the auditions I used to book. The agent made excuses for why he couldn't find work for me—and his reasons had everything to do with *my* shortcomings, not his. He began to place limits on the vision he had for me: my age became a factor for him, or my lack of expertise in a niche became an issue. All kinds of limiting factors began to crop up. Eventually, I stopped listening: my vision for myself was bigger than his. The relationship I had with this agent, regardless of how great it had once been, had run its course.

My next agent, whom I signed with a week later, booked me on three jobs in that very week. As for my old agent, I have nothing but respect for him—and he became a very successful agency mogul. We were both destined for greater things.

NEW YORK VS. L.A. VS. SMALLER MARKETS

For those of you considering a relocation, New York and L.A. are the two entertainment-industry hubs of America—but these aren't the only cities with a market for talent. The industry has always had a footprint in various cities across North America. And since the pandemic, there has been a shift toward smaller markets like Chicago, Atlanta, Miami, Dallas, Seattle, and Toronto, among others.

There are many reasons why productions are moving to these cities: space, fewer regulatory constraints, tax incentives, and affordable cost of living. Each place has its own unique culture and pathways to the business, which means that your choices are certainly not confined to New York or L.A. This may change even more drastically in the years to come, but for now let's talk about the biggest markets: New York City and L.A.

I've lived in both New York and L.A., and there are vast differences between the two for booking work. For instance, in New York you can be listed with more than one agency per category, also known as being **non-exclusive, freelance**, or **multi-listed.** For example, you could be listed with three different modeling agencies in New York, but only one in L.A. In New York, each agency will often compete for the same castings. Usually, this results in the talent taking the audition from the agent who calls about it first. Some agents in New York do not like this model, but as the saying goes: *don't hate the player, hate the game.* New York has many frustrated agents because of this highly competitive landscape, but they hustle the hardest.

In L.A., you will be expected to be **exclusive** with one agency per category (acting, modeling, or hosting). In L.A., it is standard practice to sign a contract with an agency binding you as their talent for the specific category. You'll often hear the term "signing with an agency," which simply means that the agency has added you to their list of talent—but the term is taken literally in L.A.

By signing on with too many agencies and creating the potential for a lot of casting overlap, you run the risk of burning bridges. This casting overlap is more acceptable in New York, but not in L.A. Remember what I said earlier about being future-minded? You never know when an agent will move to an agency you want to work with in the future, or even become a casting director or producer.

There's a workaround in L.A., however. Even though you are expected to be exclusive to one **mother agency**, you can have agents in Orange County and San Diego and other regions within California. It's a way to expand your footprint across multiple cities—California is a big state, after all. But if your Orange County agency wants to submit you for a casting that your mother agency in L.A. also wants to submit you for, always go with your mother agency. If your Orange County agency submits you for an L.A. casting that your mother agency *never* submitted you for, then it's fair game.

You could also cross state lines. Even though I currently reside in California, I still have agents in other states. The castings are typically regional, so your agent in Chicago won't see L.A. castings, and vice versa, unless the casting is specified to be "nationwide." And just because a casting is held in L.A. does not necessarily mean the job will be in L.A.: The casting could be in your home region, but the job could be somewhere else.

Oftentimes in these smaller market cities, and even in L.A and NYC, casting directors and agents will ask for **self-tapes** (we will cover self-tapes extensively later; for now, just know this is a pre-recorded video audition) and photos, which can be sent via platforms like WeTransfer, YouTube, or Dropbox. Sometimes, they'll just hire you for **direct bookings**. The self-tape submissions practice has further enabled talent to list with agencies across the country—and even the world.

You are not limited to the region in which you reside. Sometimes, however, the job will require you to be in the local market *if* you get the booking, so it helps to have friends or family willing to host you as a guest. If the client offers full compensation for travel and accommodation, they will specify that in the **breakdown**.

Even though you could theoretically travel the country for jobs, you will still need a home base. Where you decide to go depends on what you want. I wanted broader opportunities in modeling, which led to even broader aspirations in acting—but I worked for five years in Chicago before I made the decision to expand. In Chicago, I had the benefit of less competition and the presence of my support network, which allowed me to build my portfolio even though I wasn't necessarily making big bucks as a newbie. You can start your career right now, from anywhere—and then, if you'd like, you can take your business on the road.

INTERNATIONAL MARKETS

If you reside in a different country or are an American considering working in the international market, there are certain agencies with offices abroad. If you're looking to get into runway modeling, Milan and Paris are the primary hubs. Athens is also a good option if you are looking to build your modeling portfolio. Greece is favored by novice models for **tear-sheets** (features in editorial print). In general, Europeans seem to consume more high-gloss fashion and **lifestyle** magazines, even in our digitally inclined world.

There are similar opportunities in Asian markets. I have a friend whose L.A. agency offered her a long-term opportunity for modeling work in Japan. She lived there for a few months, and by the time she left, she had booked so much print work that she had earned a good living and came back to L.A. with a stacked portfolio. The opportunities are there, even if you are early in your career. It all depends on how far you are willing to travel and the type of work you are interested in doing.

Whether you are looking to travel short-term or make a long-term move overseas, technology has enabled talent to have more reach in otherwise unreachable places. There are truly more possibilities for expansion now.

UNION VS. NON-UNION

When I was starting out with agencies, my goal was to become part of a **union**. SAG/AFTRA is the union for television and film actors and advocates the interests of its members in negotiations and contracts with studios. There is no similar union for modeling/print work, but there is a union for the commercial, theatrical, and hosting sectors, as well as a non-union category for those roles. While I do appreciate some of the benefits of being in a union—like the health benefits available to those actors who book a certain dollar amount per year—there is plenty of non-union work out there, now more than ever.

There are advantages and disadvantages to both union and non-union work. In a non-union contract, you get paid for the day and you receive a **buyout**. A buyout is a lump sum negotiated by your agent that depends on the length of time this commercial/episode/segment will air. When you are union, you are typically compensated with **residuals**. This means you get paid every time something airs, even if it re-airs years and years down the line.

But even with residuals, there's usually fine print you need to pay attention to for union contracts. Have a trusted advisor who is familiar with contracts review the documents if you can. Even when you have an agent, make sure to always read every word of your contract. I know it's exciting to get your first contract signed and sealed because it means you're moving one step closer to your dreams, but you may inadvertently sign up for something that will be a nightmare down the road.

You may have an agent who is incredible at contracts that notices some red flags on a gig and tries to talk you out of a deal that they think is unfair. Even though they have your best interest at heart, it's okay to trust your instincts and override their advice in certain circumstances. If you feel that the role has potential for a greater upside in the future, you could override your agent. You two are on a team, yes—but you are inevitably going to be viewing deals from two different angles.

You will learn over time if union or non-union work is more suitable for you. This will depend on so many factors, especially if you work in television and film. **Always do your research, use your instincts, and read the fine print.**

THE AGENCY SPLIT

You will pay nothing upfront when signing on with an agency: instead, agents make their money when you get booked. For non-union work, expect the agency commission to be about 15-20% of your paycheck from a booking. In union work, the agency commission is 10%. For modeling/print jobs, the commission is 20%.

From an IRS perspective, some jobs are classified as 1099, which means you work as a contractor and pay taxes on your earnings—like a freelancer. Some other jobs are classified as W-2's: for instance, if you book a role on television or film, you may be considered an employee of the production company (usually simply referred to as the **production**). In these cases, taxes and agency fees are paid out by the production, and you'll keep the net amount after your agency commission is deducted.

If you can, hire an accountant. Remember: you are a business. Keep all pay stubs and receipts and update your ledger often. Any costs associated with your business, which includes gas mileage, website, reels, headshots, hair/makeup for a shoot, and more, should be recorded and evaluated for their potential deductibility.

MANAGERS

A manager is an advisor. They are different from an agent in that they can offer you more big-picture career advice and will typically tap into their personal networks to get you in front of a different set of people. The role of a manager is to enhance your career and maximize your opportunities. You probably won't need a manager in the early stages—but others in the industry might tell you that it's never too early for a manager. I have friends who hired a manager before they even signed on with an agent.

What are some reasons these friends had for hiring a manager? A manager, like an agent, only gets paid when you book a job. A good manager will go the extra mile to pitch you to clients, get you auditions or meetings, and sing your praises all over town. Some people prefer to work with managers because they offer a more personal relationship, with more frequent one-on-one meetings and phone calls. They generally have fewer clients than an agent and are therefore able to give you more of their undivided attention.

Typically, someone will hire a manager long after they've been working with agents and are consistently booking jobs. A manager retains a commission of 10-20%. Those people who have an agent and a manager will have to pay both, even if it was just the agent who booked them a job. In my experience, I believe you should hire a manager if it seems right to you: if, for instance, you need help finding a good agent or if you are booking so many jobs that you need extra attention. But if you have an agent working hard for you, that may be more than enough for now.

BANDWAGON FANS

This is the term I have chosen to use for agents and managers who try to pounce on your already established success. Be wary of these types. A manager once approached me and delivered a showy pitch on how he could get me in front of bigger and better television opportunities, and in exchange he would take a cut of my earnings from a show I was already on, and previously booked with no help from him. I rejected him before he finished his sentence.

Why would I ever sacrifice a portion of success I already had in place for theoretical future success? You will likely encounter scenarios that require you to take risks, but any agent or manager who suggests taking your existing earnings is offering you a bad deal.

THE NO-AGENT ROUTE

There are undeniable benefits to having an agent. An agent has an established network in the industry. A good agent will be on top of all the fine print in a contract and will negotiate on your behalf, and a great agent will help you to improve your craft. That said, you may still decide that you'd like to go the agentless route.

If you choose to go agentless, you need to be self-submitting every day. You'll start by creating a profile on casting sites like Casting Frontier, Casting Networks, and Actors Access and including all your photos, reels, and other relevant materials on these profiles. From there, you can set up alerts for general roles that are a potential fit (e.g., voice-over roles, roles for women 40-55, or hosting roles). And when you receive the alerts, you'll submit yourself.

Even if you do get yourself an agent and/or manager, you will always need to be your own best advocate. You will still need to read your own contracts and set up your own alerts for suitable roles, and you'll still self-submit from time to time. Your agent may decide to only submit you for jobs that pay over $500, but if you need a quick $200, self-submit on those casting sites.

An agent is there to help you book new opportunities and to act as an advisor—but do not misunderstand this to mean you can sit back and relax. You're still the one doing the heavy lifting here. The agent is there to spot you.

CHECKPOINT:

- Research agencies: look at their website and social media.
- Remember names. Take notes in a notebook or on a spreadsheet.
- Understand what you'll need to make your submissions and look out for local open calls.
- Submit snapshots and résumés according to submission guidelines.
- Prepare for your business. Create a ledger to record your expenses and earnings.

THREE

PHOTOS AND REELS
(OR BODY OF WORK)

H ere's an exercise you can do right now at home. Look in the mirror. Smile wide. Now be dramatic. Now give me a doctor look. Give me a cop look. Now you're in a rom-com: you play a hopeless small-town romantic who has just moved to the big city. This exercise seems funny and unnecessary, but this is exactly what you will be doing for your photos. The casting directors will want to see your versatility: that you can be convincing as a medical professional, or a serious detective, or a soap opera diva.

YOUR MINDSET AT A SHOOT

As I was writing this section about photos, I confided to a friend that it felt too instructional. Yes, there is the business aspect of these photos—they are your calling cards and your entryway to the clients. But is that their only purpose?

This friend asked me, "How do you feel when you're having your photos taken?" I hadn't thought about the *feeling* until then. But when I did, I realized that the process is invigorating. As you step into the various wardrobes and as you channel your different characters, you experience a process of discovery: one that uncovers abilities and aspects of your personality that perhaps you never expressed before.

This is a culmination of a lifetime of observing others, of interacting with people in your daily life, of simply paying attention. Taking on a persona is a creative endeavor. Sure, you will be following the photographer's direction—but you are the artist, and you must leave any personal issues and insecurities at the door, because they will show through on camera.

To this day, I can look at certain photos and remember the life moments I was experiencing at the time. I can tell which photos were taken during hard times and which were taken during happy times in my life. Once you can get out of your head and become fully engaged in the shoot, your photos will showcase your versatility.

YOUR FIRST PHOTOS

Your first photos will be guided by your agent. The process of obtaining professional photos will be so much easier after an agency has agreed to represent you. They will provide you with a list of photographers, and you'll research the best fit according to costs, look, vibe, and other aspects important to you. Check out their website and Instagram: you will notice how each photographer is different in terms of style and direction.

You'll see what I mean as you browse through the websites of various photographers. One very popular photographer with whom I've worked in the past has a style unique to him: he will position the shot in an off-center way and use bold and vibrant color schemes in his backgrounds. Good photographers all have their own set of beliefs about the right way to capture you.

Pay attention to the models themselves, including their poses and appearance. You will be where they are, being asked to pose and present yourself. The more closely you pay attention to these nuances, the better prepared you will be, and the more comfortable you will become at your shoots.

When you start booking jobs and showing up to actual shoots, you will be directed to pose, express your personality, and move in a certain way. This applies to models as well as actors. Getting in front of a photographer is the first rehearsal you'll have.

Photographers, importantly, know what an agency wants and expects. They will be instrumental in guiding you through the process of photo selection. Once you have chosen a photographer, set up an initial appointment for the shoot. Ask the photographer for their hair/makeup recommendations. I suggest using one of their contacts, because they've worked together over time and have established a rhythm.

These photos create your first impression. They are expensive, yes, but they are important. I cannot stress enough the importance of good hair and makeup.

Please don't misunderstand this to mean you should look done-up and decked out, though. Here's the big secret—you should look as natural as possible. Think of hair and makeup as helping you to look as best as possible in your most natural state. Take my word for it: casting directors will expect the person arriving to audition to look like the person they picked out of the stack, not a completely different version of that person.

They want you to look like your photos unless otherwise specified. If they want you to come dressed as a glam rockstar, they will explicitly request this. In those cases, dress the part or as close as you can (we will talk more about this in the Auditions section).

You will also need to bring various outfits to the shoot. Clothing choices should come from discussions between you and your agent and you and your photographer. Listen to what they advise. Remember, each agency represents different types of roles, so they will have great input here. They may advise you to bring more basic outfits, business-professional looks like suits, or edgy/chic wear—it all depends on which roles you and your agent have discussed.

Nowadays, all photography is done with a digital camera—this means you can ask to see the first few photos to see how everything looks. Once you see yourself in those first few shots, this will help to guide you on what is and isn't working. Are your photos representing you the way you want? The way your agent advised? You can be proactive in this initial round.

Anytime you feel uncomfortable or unsure, don't be afraid to ask. You have professionals around you—learn from them. You will learn how your look shifts in studio lighting and outdoor lighting, against different kinds of backdrops, or from different angles. Everyone has an optimal light and backdrop specific to them. You will learn so much about your own camera persona.

The photographers will guide you and give you tips, but that does not mean you should be afraid to express yourself and ask questions. Pay attention to all of this and be present. This is not just a step in the process, this is *the* process. Your business is to be in front of the camera.

PHOTOGRAPHY COSTS

Photography is priced based on the number of looks. For a basic photoshoot, expect to spend $300–$500. A hair and makeup person will cost you another couple hundred dollars. Prices vary widely depending on your city, how many looks you shoot, and the popularity of the photographer and the hair and makeup people. You don't need to pick the most expensive people—the important thing is that you are comfortable and feel good about the process.

PORTFOLIOS

Portfolios are especially important for those of you considering a career in modeling. Think of your portfolio as you would think about yourself: always changing, adapting, evolving. It should showcase your versatility. As we discussed earlier, your first photos will look natural, with you modeling in various expressions and wardrobes. Over time, your portfolio may evolve to include bolder photos showing off some bigger looks. As you gain more experience, the client—in addition to agents and photographers—will shape your portfolio.

Actors use **headshots** (from the shoulder up) and can include three-quarter shots (from the waist up) as well, depending on the market you are in and the current trends.

Modeling is a bit more nuanced. Your portfolio can have face shots, **beauty shots**, and full-body shots. For those of you who are interested in modeling, you will need an Instagram account and website. If you already have an Instagram account, you may want to change it up to include more modeling-specific photos. You can still include those shots of you running a 10k, or that candid one of you laughing it up at a concert—these can be strategically included to show off your personality but try to keep it professional. Include shots from your sessions with your photographer.

Agencies, casting directors, and clients will most certainly be looking at your Instagram. Many of these clients will use your social media accounts as a test for your cultural alignment with their company. My advice is to be mindful of every photo you post: ask yourself if this is how you wish to represent yourself to different clients.

Some agencies will ask you to prepare a **portfolio book**. A book includes both a physical portfolio book and a corresponding online version. Oftentimes, your agency will provide the cover with their logo, with plastic sleeves inside. This is for your various looks and previous print work (once you accumulate them).

COMP CARDS VS. ZED CARDS

Depending on which city you are working in, an agency may ask you to prepare a **comp card** (New York) or **zed card** (L.A.). These are outdated terms, as most agencies have gone digital, but there are still agencies that ask you to have them. This is basically just a large photo card with your main photo on one side and a series of four photos showing off various looks on the other side. The comp/zed cards will also have your name and agency printed, your measurements, and any union affiliation.

DIVERSE LOOKS

When I started my modeling career in Chicago, I often heard that my olive skin and Mediterranean features were "too ethnic" for some clients. At the time, the in-demand look was "American girl next door." It wasn't until I moved to New York that I was exposed to more opportunities. In New York, the "exotic" look was on the rise. During that time, I booked a print ad for a Mediterranean yogurt brand and I was also featured in a Latin Pop music video.

These days, clients get very specific with their desired look: if they are looking for someone to play the role of a Mexican-American character, they will very likely hire a Mexican-American actor. I can recall a time as early as 2005 when there was a casting call for three models representing three different nationalities: one Spanish, one Italian, and one French. The three of us who were hired were coincidentally all Greek, apparently because our look was "close enough" to what the client was looking for. Today, things have changed: there is a culture of authentic representation now. The industry is more inclusive than ever—so if you identify with a cultural heritage, include it in your story.

These days, there is also more demand for real people, real looks, and "non-traditional types." When I worked on the original *Deal or No Deal*, the models varied across skin tones, hair color, and height—but each of us otherwise looked like a conventional model you'd expect to see on television at the time. The more recent reboot in 2018 called for a truly diverse group of women that included all shapes and sizes, ethnicities, and even backgrounds—including models that had no prior modeling experience whatsoever. The reboot prided itself on being a celebration of women and happened around the time the industry was starting to have important conversations around diversity.

The entertainment world is highly reflective of society, and the only message here is to feel free to highlight those unconventional aspects of yourself that previously may have been underrepresented in the industry.

REELS

A **reel** is a video sample of your acting work meant to convince the casting directors and acting agents of two things:

1) you have talent, and 2) you have experience.

But how do I get my reel together if I haven't booked any jobs? I mentioned the importance of taking on small jobs earlier, and I will reiterate that here: find speaking roles in local plays or student films—anything that can showcase your acting talent. Your pursuit of small jobs doesn't have to stop just because you've signed with an agent. Although your reel should include roles you have actually booked, a last-resort option is to create a self-tape. You can do this at home or—if you have the budget—in a professional studio.

As long as you can demonstrate that you have talent, a casting director or acting agent may overlook a low-budget production, provided there is good-quality lighting and sound with no distractions or background noise, and you are the production's focal point. There are many video-editing tools available, and YouTube is a great place to find tutorials on how to optimize these tools. Again, if you have the budget, I recommend having a professional help you to edit your video reel.

If you have little to no material for your reel, here are some steps to creating a DIY self-tape. Even if you have some work under your belt, it may be worth it to get in the practice of creating a self-tape audition. Again, this is your way of presenting your acting talent, so you'll want to practice and prepare like you would any presentation/audition.

DIY SELF-TAPE FOR REELS

Step 1: Pick a couple of scenes from a play/television show/movie, one that has **dialogue** with another character and one **monologue**.

Step 2: Memorize and rehearse your lines.

Step 3: Style yourself. Who is the character you are playing, and how would they show up to this scene? You are interpreting the writer here—think about your interpretation of the material.

Step 4: Set the stage. Pick a quiet, well-lit room indoors with natural light (avoid the outdoors—too much background noise). Play around with different lighting scenarios to see how the camera captures you in the light. If you want to take a minimalist approach, set up a white backdrop with minimal props, like a single chair. The staging area should complement what you are trying to achieve with the scene. A ring light is a great investment for self-tape lighting.

Step 5: Set up a camera on a fixed tripod or stand. Make sure the angle works. Play around with the modes. Oftentimes for self-tape auditions, they ask you to record in landscape format.

Step 6: Press record, act out the scene, stop record, and repeat.

If you have previously done some theater or camera work, and if it demonstrates your talent and experience, find a copy. It's not always easy to obtain, and it may require some phone calls and emails to track down the person who could send it to you, but the footage could be helpful for your reel.

Try to collect as much of your work as possible. I regret not collecting more of my work when I was starting out—I hated seeing myself on camera and hearing my voice, so I just avoided it. But watching your performances is not only helpful for your reel—it's necessary for your improvement. You know how sports coaches review plays frame by frame with the players? Same goes for acting. Get into an open, non-judgmental, and analytical mindset and review your work. Don't criticize yourself, don't get emotional—just watch and learn for the sake of improvement.

If you can hone the process of analyzing your work early, your initial reel will present well. A general rule of thumb is to keep them short, about 1–2 minutes. Less is more! The reel should have snippets of your work—do not add entire pieces that drag on and on. The reel is meant for casting directors and acting agents to get a general idea of you as an actor.

Try to show off your versatility across different characters and genres. As with your photo portfolios, you want your reel to show casting directors that you can do well in a serious role and just as well in a comedic role. You'll want to put your best stuff at the start of the reel. Sometimes the casting directors and acting agents will only see your first few seconds, especially if they have hundreds of other reels to review. If you can captivate them in the first few seconds, they may continue onto the rest—or they may be captivated at first, only to change their minds.

So far, we have talked about your first-ever reel. To recap, this is what you will use to get signed by an acting-specific agent, who will then forward the reel to casting directors. Once you're signed, your agent may direct your reel, like how they direct photos. And you will inevitably add to your reel as you compile more acting work.

If you start going after certain types of jobs—hosting jobs, for example—you will have to put together a hosting-specific reel. Nothing changes with regards to the length of the reel and the high quality you should be striving for—the only thing that will change is the material. You'll want to prepare by understanding what it is you are hosting and to address the camera directly, as hosts do. And you'll want to do your homework, like you did before, by watching game shows and reality shows and studying the hosts.

Just how important is a good reel? A really good reel could get you a direct booking, where the casting director or client hires you based on the reel alone, bypassing the audition or self-tape altogether.

RÉSUMÉ

If you intend to pursue acting and hosting jobs, you will need a résumé. This is for your agent, casting directors, and clients. It is not unlike a traditional résumé, but it should be tailored to you as a performing artist. Please research resume templates to make sure they are industry specific. On the casting sites, there is a place for you to add your résumé and samples of your work, and there are also fields for adding experience and skills manually. As you input your previous job experience, there will be fields where you'll want to enter the **director's** name and the year.

A note: if you've done previous commercial work, just indicate "Commercials: list available upon request." It's a standard expectation that your specific commercial and print ad work will be left off a résumé—but standards change all the time, so make sure you consult your agent and industry friends on the latest protocols.

Just like your reel and your portfolio, the résumé should be updated with every new job you book—and don't skip the skills section. Make sure to include if you are a beginner, intermediate, or advanced. Indicate any relevant subsets—flamenco dancer vs. break-dancer. Another sought-after résumé skill is reading from a teleprompter. Pay attention to newscasts and see if you can notice if the host is using a teleprompter. Get creative—if you have a motorcycle license, put that on there. Even if you think your love of windsurfing is irrelevant, include it. You never know what could be useful.

For example, I once booked an Old Navy commercial because of my formal education in dance. In another life, I taught children how to dance. On my résumé, I included this as well as my experience freestyle-dancing from my days doing choreographed routines with my girlfriends at Excalibur Club in Chicago back in the 90s. Every detail matters.

Your résumé skills are also important to casting sites—we'll talk more about this in the next chapter about auditions. I recommend that you start building your résumé with whatever you can. Include your small jobs (Chapter 1), your skills, and your training. And don't worry if you see a lot of blank space now as you are starting out—it's a good exercise in getting you in the professional-actor mindset.

CHECKPOINT:

- Get photo ready. Play around with different looks and poses in the mirror.
- Start reaching out to photographers and hair and makeup people.
- Do some homework. Watch movies and shows. Look at print ads. Notice what you like and ask yourself why.
- Build your résumé.
- Build your reel and portfolio

FOUR

AUDITIONS

You're gathering your photos, building your reels, and generally being a boss. In the meantime, your agent is sifting through descriptions of various roles, called breakdowns, from casting directors. For example, *brunette female aged 25–35.* The client and casting directors will usually be specific about the look and type they want. Sometimes they will be vaguer, like *mom-type,* other times they will be *very* specific, like *big motorcycle guy with face piercings.* Sometimes your agent will submit you for a role even if you aren't a perfect match on paper because they see an aspect in you that they think will work for the role. Once your agent submits you for a role, your photos, résumé, and videos all get in front of the casting directors—or, most likely at this point, their assistants.

The casting directors and/or their assistants then sift through the many submissions from all the different agencies to narrow down a talent list to invite to audition.

If a casting director invites you to audition, expect to receive a text and/or email asking for confirmation. If you decline, be prepared to give a reason. Keep in mind that your agent is going to bat for you and expects you to show up to the audition. In fact, your number-one responsibility at this stage is going to auditions. Sometimes you'll get a super-last-minute audition—you're still expected to make it. Some of my best jobs came from last-minute auditions or gigs. Seize an opportunity when it comes your way. And if you take too long to confirm, you may lose your spot.

Auditioning is a full-time job. You are a business, not a side hustle, after all. I have some friends who work in hospitality to pay the bills while they get their businesses off the ground, and they would all tell you that it's an exhausting juggling act. They've made it work by taking evening and weekend shifts in order to free up their mornings and afternoons. If you absolutely must work another job, you must still make your auditions the priority.

The audition begins before you even walk into the audition room. You will have some time to review a job (called an **audition ticket**) before an audition. In the breakdown, they will typically give you a general wardrobe description and "vibe."

Here is a sample audition ticket:
Project type: Commercial
Role name: Working out woman/gym
Role type: Principal
Description: She doesn't have to be in amazing shape, but with her workouts it's looking that way.
Age: 45–50
Wardrobe: Casual/fit
Synopsis: There will be no dialogue: this is a slice-of-life production with snippets
Rate: $500 for 10 hours + $1,500 Buyout
There are three major websites that agents use to coordinate with casting directors: Casting Network (castingnetworks.com), the parent network of L.A. Casting and New York Casting; Cast-

ing Frontier; and Actors Access. You are responsible for creating your profile on each one of these sites, and you will need to add your agency code to link your agent with your profile. Here, you will add your photos and reels, as well as your skills and talents.

Also, keep your **IMDB** profile updated with your most recent work and photos. If you've done previous work, the studios will credit you and that **credit** will appear on your IMDB. But you must add your own résumé, photos, reels, clips, personal videos, and other related information. All these websites are paid services, but they are very important for your visibility and worth the expense.

The audition ticket I used as an example earlier seems pretty straightforward, right? *Workout woman.* Show up in activewear, project a spirit of fun and fitness—piece of cake. But there are some tricks of the trade that I will share with you. For auditions, you'll never want to wear white, because you'll most likely get washed out with the backdrop. You'll want to wear bright colors—but avoid patterns. You could go the extra mile and wear something with the client's brand color.

I'll tell you a not-so-surprising secret: I booked the most jobs when I walked in with confidence. Not arrogance. The good-mood-nothing-can-bring-me-down kind of vibe. At times, that simply meant I walked in with a take-it-or-leave-it attitude— maybe I had a lot going on at the time, or there was a different part I wanted more. Either way, it's funny looking back at the times I really tried and the times I didn't—and in both cases, the important element I brought to the audition was *confidence.*

In the audition ticket, you will also receive lines if the gig includes a speaking part. Usually, the lines will be posted at the audition, but bring a copy to work on while you wait for your turn in the lobby. If it's a bigger role—with another actor in the scene, for instance—you will want to bring a paper copy into the audition with you.

Please try to memorize as much as possible; this will keep you in the moment, and you'll present more authentically when you have practiced and absorbed the character. There are coaches out there who can help you with the audition process specifically. They may even prepare you for unexpected scenarios—like receiving a last-minute copy (also called **sides**) of your lines. This is called a **cold read**.

AT THE AUDITION

When you arrive at an audition, there will be a casting assistant checking everyone in. There will be a sign-in sheet, where you'll include your name, agent's name, role, time of arrival, and appointment time. There are different sign-in sheets depending on your union affiliation. These days, it's common to scan a QR code that links to a sign-in sheet to complete on your phone. Oftentimes, you'll be prompted to fill out a **size card**, or size sheet, where you'll enter your details and agency info as well as your measurements, hair color, eye color, and social media handles.

Sometimes, if the casting team is running behind schedule, they will ask you to audition with a few other actors. For modeling auditions, once you're in the audition room, it's typically a bit quicker. They will interview you in front of the camera, asking you questions to get a sense of your personality. "What's your favorite food?" "Where was the last place you traveled?"

Regardless of the type of audition, you'll walk into the room and stand where they tell you, usually marked by an X on the floor. Then they will direct you. They'll ask you to **slate** your name and ask you who your agent is. They'll cue you when the camera starts rolling.

These days, everything is digital and clients most likely won't require a hard copy of your photo and résumé—but bring them anyway. Some casting directors are old-school like that. Be prepared for anything, especially if it will help you to stand out.

Before you even walk into the building, leave your life worries outside. This is your job; this is your business. You are presenting to a client, and you got here because you are a professional, and because you were invited. When you walk into the waiting area, you will get a sense of the energy. Pay attention and stay in the moment. Is it quiet? Is it social? Does it feel like you are at the doctor's office waiting for an appointment?

After you have checked in, and you know you are in the right place, the waiting begins. As you wait, prepare for your audition if there are lines. If you feel nervous, do some breathing exercises, count to ten, listen to music—do anything that will soothe you and get you in an authentic headspace. Trust in all the work you have done to get here. There will be other people there competing for the same job. Don't let this intimidate you. Take a quick scan, and then get back to you.

And make sure you've had something to eat! Never go into an audition hungry. I always like to have water and a snack on me for days I'm running from audition to audition. I have bombed because of an empty tank. Take every measure to prepare your mind, body, and consciousness for an audition—not just because you want to perform well, but because there is no worse feeling than walking out of an audition and feeling the *coulda-shoulda-wouldas*. There are forces beyond your control in the casting process, but how you audition is the one thing you *can* control. The more you audition, the better you should get at developing a ***feel-your-best, think-your-best, do-your-best attitude***.

Momentum is key to becoming an audition pro. I can tell you exactly when I started improving in the early days: when I stopped harping on bad auditions or rejections and instead decided to keep going. Keep moving and hustling. I completed an audition and immediately forgot about it afterward. I focused on the next audition. That doesn't mean I stopped preparing or trying—I just stopped getting hung up on one role. I played the volume game.

That was the turning point. Even when I bombed—and I mean, I've truly bombed so hard I saw the look of horror on the faces of the casting directors and their assistants—I kept going. I once had an audition after working on a major network show for many years and I stumbled over my lines. I felt so self-conscious, so out of practice and out of place. And this was me at the height of my career—*I'm a pro*, I thought. *Why is this happening?* I was out of practice. I had been out of the audition process for such a long time. I had lost my momentum.

SELF-TAPE

Pre-pandemic, only some studios requested self-tape auditions. During the pandemic, self-tapes became standard practice—and now, they are here to stay.

The self-tape audition works exactly like a traditional in-person audition, except that you will be performing at home, in front of a camera. Once you receive your audition ticket, prepare your at-home set and camera like you would in a DIY reel. The audition ticket will contain specific instructions. For certain modeling and commercial self-tapes, they may ask to see both the front and back of your hands. They may ask you to state your height. Other times, they will have you show your profile, or answer certain questions into the camera. Follow these instructions as close to the letter as possible—and don't forget to **slate** your name! (Introduce yourself give any other information the casting director is asking for).

The primary advantage of a self-tape is the ability to revise. You have unlimited takes, whereas an in-person audition may limit your takes to two or three. Once your self-tape is ready, you will upload it according to the instructions provided, usually through a third-party file transfer platform but sometimes directly to the casting site.

THE CALLBACK

For print ads and modeling in general, the casting team will make their decision based on one **casting** or **go-see**. For commercials, television, and film, there is a **callback** process. The casting team will narrow down the actors they like for the role. If they choose you, they will invite you back to audition again. Sometimes, the audition is in the exact same format as the first one; other times, they will have noted some changes. Either way, it is known as a callback audition.

When you get a callback, wear the same exact thing you did to the first audition unless otherwise noted—if they liked it the first time, they'll like it the second time. For the most part. I once got a callback for a commercial in which the first audition instructed us to wear workout clothes, but the callback audition asked for casual clothes. Wires were crossed between the agent and casting team, and I was never informed—so I showed up wearing my little bike shorts and sports bra while everyone else wore jeans and blouses.

I stood in front of everyone, including the client and casting team, dropped my bags and just said, "Welp, guess I didn't get the memo…" and everyone erupted in laughter. I must have made an impression, because I ended up booking the part. I didn't even mean to be funny—the comment just came out of my mouth. If anything, I was annoyed with the situation. The point is, there are so many rules and protocols, but ultimately, they are booking you because you stand out to them—for a reason that will often be completely unknown to you.

VIRTUAL AUDITIONS

Virtual auditions are becoming increasingly common. Your first audition will either be an in-person audition or self-tape, and typically so will your callback. But these days, your callback audition may be virtual. The casting director sends a link, and the audition begins as a meeting between you, the director, and the client. After introductions, you'll perform in front of the camera. The guidelines will have been provided ahead of the virtual audition.

A virtual audition is not unlike an in-person audition, where they both happen in real time, so the same advice applies. Just like an in-person audition, you will have several takes with notes from the casting director. The difference between a virtual audition and a self-tape is that a self-tape can be edited until you are satisfied, whereas a virtual audition happens on the casting director's terms. The industry is evolving, and I believe that we will see the audition process continue to move toward the virtual space.

SCREEN TEST

For certain television shows and movies, you may get multiple callbacks, depending on the job. The ultimate callback after the casting team has selected a final list of candidates is called a **screen test**. You won't always have to screen test for a part: this depends on the job and its specific casting protocol. But if you are asked to screen test, prepare for it like you are preparing for the job itself. You will have received lines ahead of time, usually part of a scene with another actor. Make sure to memorize these lines just like you would for the actual job. The production will provide the hair and makeup and instruct you on what to wear.

The screen test is exactly that—a test of your screen presence. Screen tests also exist to assess your chemistry with the other actors booked for the project. If it's a screen test for a hosting job, you will perform similarly—as though you were hosting the show. There is no room for error here, as your screen test is as close as you'll come to being aired to the public without actually airing.

Everyone who is involved in the production will watch the screen tests: the network people, producers, directors, even the hair and makeup people. The entire crew has a front-row view. This can be nerve-wracking—remember, just do your job. You are a professional; you are a business. And the studio is a business, too. In life, you will be forgiven for your mistakes. In this business, the threshold for forgiveness shrinks the higher you get in the callback process.

I've had good screen tests, and I've had bad screen tests. I once got so far in the audition and callback process, right up to rehearsing with the director, and nailing it, just to bomb the screen test. I started shaking. I was way-off balance. My fear took hold and did not let go. It's like that camera had it out for me and shot laser beams to throw me off. It was early in my career, and I just couldn't handle the pressure. I wanted the part so badly. I was so tightly wound it squeezed the confidence right out of me.

It happens to the best of us. If I am to draw a lesson out of this, it's that you cannot get attached to a part. Just like in business, there is so little room for emotion. Don't misunderstand this to mean that you should stop caring altogether, or that you should become cold and hardened. It means that you should never get attached to a single job, whether you get it or not—that even in your highest triumph, or what you might think of as your lowest failure, you must keep moving forward. This is what will make you a professional. And as a friend once told me, "You wanna be a pro? Act like a pro."

A screen test is a high-stakes audition—there is no sugarcoating it. If you have reached this point, take it as a sign that you are doing all the right things and try your best. Everything we have discussed, all the work you have done, will have led you to the screen test. But also take comfort in knowing that a screen test will not make or break your career.

That screen test I bombed was just a lost business deal. I

moved on, and I was rewarded for my tenacity later down the road. The best was yet to come.

CHECKPOINT:

- Prepare for auditions by rehearsing lines or interviews at home.
- Document your measurements somewhere handy.
- Set up your tech and email inbox so that you never miss an audition ticket.

FIVE

REJECTION

ou will be rejected. You will experience dimensions of rejection you never knew were possible. You will be rejected by agents, casting directors, clients, even when you have been signed by an agent, even when you had your best audition and impressed all the decision-makers, even after you have already booked the job. If you absolutely cannot accept rejection, and I mean really accept it, I cannot help you. I can only help you reframe rejection.

The first time I ever experienced professional rejection was the hardest. It was a beauty pageant, and I wanted to win so badly. I created this false belief in my young mind that this competition was somehow a make-or-break moment. I lost, and I was crushed. The second time, also a beauty pageant, I lost again—but I did not perceive it as a rejection. The difference was simply this: the second time around, I made a point to have fun and make friends.

When I made a purposeful switch to just relaxing and enjoying the environment and the experience, I let go of the outcome. I had no expectations. By the third pageant, I had fun *and* placed in the top five. Rejection became something entirely different; it became another part of the experience that wasn't good or bad. It was as integral to the process as showing up.

Later in my career, I experienced a more high-stakes version of this in auditions and screen tests. I mentioned this earlier when I talked about momentum, but when I was auditioning nonstop, I didn't have time to think about landing roles. I had to think about preparing for and getting to auditions. I auditioned constantly, which meant I was constantly rejected. But it also meant I sometimes booked jobs. You see? Many auditions + many rejections = jobs. Even the most seasoned actors get rejected.

You will be rejected for reasons that have nothing to do with you or your talent. It's frustrating when the reason why you were not hired is not revealed to you, but 99 times out of 100, it will remain unknown. You may be rejected because you flat-out bombed. Do not waste your time feeling sorry for yourself or kicking yourself. Unlike the previous type of rejection, where you have no idea why you were not picked, bombing is something you can learn from.

You may be rejected because someone simply had more Instagram followers than you. You may be rejected because of consensus, where five out of ten people loved you, but the other five loved someone else, and as a compromise they ended up picking someone entirely different. It can become maddening—if you let it. Remember: auditioning is a full-time job, and part of the job means not being hired.

The moment you begin to desire something, you naturally create an expectation, and expectation is the root of the pain of rejection. But if you can learn to focus on the process—that unending cycle of practice, preparation, presence, and let's add another p for positivity—you will not only have more fun, but you will also naturally become a better professional.

I will warn you: you will hear comments about your look. I've lost jobs because I was "too ethnic," "too skinny," because I had a "big ass," because I had a "big nose," or because I was "too short." When I was *thirty*, I was told I was "too old." Some people will hear something like this and run out to get a surgical procedure. Others will unfortunately develop eating disorders. This is the dark side of the industry that can, and often does, cause serious damage.

I've seen people react to these sorts of comments by going under the knife, only to be told they look fake or just like everyone else with the Snapchat filter look—not to mention the mental and physical effects associated with botched cosmetic surgery. We should all be appreciating our differences instead of trying to look more alike. Perfection doesn't exist—and striving for perfection won't get you roles.

FAMILY AND FRIENDS

Rejection may even come from your loved ones. Your family and friends won't always understand the business. They may try to discourage you, intentionally or unintentionally—but you'll know if it's coming from a good place, and usually it is. It helps to explain the process to your nearest and dearest so that they have a chance to get on board. Remember that what they know about the entertainment industry is likely coming from what they've seen on TV or read about in the tabloids.

My traditional Greek mother saw my first swimsuit ad and cried—she got the wrong impression that I would only be featured in revealing shoots. But as I explained my work and even invited her to the set during one of my jobs on a soap opera, she saw the degree of professionalism among the cast and crew. I was able to convince my toughest critic.

Get your people on board. Tell them what you're going through. Give them a chance to root for you. Ultimately, you will need to figure out who you are on your own. When I was starting out in Chicago, it was hard to tune out the noise from my friends and family, regardless of how encouraging or constructive they were. Too much advice and feedback, especially from people who haven't been through it, can be a detriment.

It took going to New York and focusing on my career for me to notice how susceptible I had been to other people's opinions. Those thoughts had been getting in the way of my growth. I'm not suggesting that you remove yourself from your support network, but it would help to ask them to be supportive—and sometimes that means staying out of your way.

CONFIDENCE

Confidence is the hardest trait to teach someone. There are so many moments in our lives, beginning in childhood, that have led to how we view ourselves—and social media has only complicated this further. We all have our insecurities. Picture the biggest movie star in your mind: that person has experienced plenty of self-doubt.

I have found that the most effective way to quiet my negative thoughts is to stop comparing myself to others. I am most confident when I remember I am a work in progress with plenty to offer, rather than someone who is better or worse than another person.

Other people's opinions of you have nothing to do with you—other people have nothing to do with you, period. In this business, you will be competing for jobs with others who are on their own path, one that could be similar to yours but also could be very different. Your peers will come from various backgrounds and situations.

We all have something unique to offer, and there are enough jobs to go around, truly. Take on a spirit of camaraderie and build people up when you can, rather than undermine them. Your turn will come, and when it does, won't it be nice to have friends to congratulate you?

You will experience arrogant types in this business. *Arrogance stems from insecurity.* Say that sentence repeatedly until it sticks. Humility is unpopular in Hollywood, that's true. There are many people who believe that they must trample over others in order to get their way, or that their value lies only in how they look and who they know. But even in this business, good guys finish first—in the long run, at least. Be grateful to everyone who helps you and remember who they are. Repay their kindness and pay their kindness forward.

Be grateful even to those who give you an opportunity that falls through. You can't always control an outcome, but you can certainly acknowledge the people who gave you a chance—even a small one. Trust me when I say, in this business, arrogant and superficial types are a dime a dozen, but true kindness and a spirit of generosity will stand out.

I realize I cannot teach kindness, that's way beyond my pay grade. So, if it doesn't come naturally to you, at the very least say thank you (and try to mean it) and look people in the eye when you speak to them.

I know I've said a lot about rejection, but you will need to figure out how to make your own armor. I can only tell you to take care of your mind, body, and spirit. I can only tell you to surround yourself with good people—and to spend your money wisely (more on that in the next chapter). Some of the best businesses out there came out of failure better and stronger. Be *that* business.

CHECKPOINT:

- Build your rejection armor.
- Ask your family and friends for support, but take their advice selectively.
- Consult a professional if you need help with body image.

SIX

MIND, BODY, SPIRIT...AND MONEY

In the fast-paced, high-stakes environment of the entertainment industry, having healthy outlets is imperative. I emphasized the importance of eating before an audition, and I will tell you that a healthy diet is going to have both a visible and internal positive effect. The last thing you want is to show up to an audition or job looking gaunt and pale and feeling blah. You can achieve a healthy glow by eating more fruits and vegetables, sleeping well, and avoiding alcohol as much as possible. Maintain an exercise regimen—I personally love (very) long walks and dancing. These activities are not just a means to an end to keep my body in shape. They are necessary for me to get into a good headspace.

You don't have to strive to look like one of the Amazonians in *Wonder Woman* or one of the Spartan guys in *300*. All types of figures are being represented in the media today. A fit body is now more in demand than a thin body. The point is to stay healthy—that means body *and* mind. Body acceptance is a hot topic, and I'm very happy to see that things have changed, in that actors and models no longer feel the need to starve themselves to work in the field. There are so many gorgeous curvy and full-figured professionals crushing it in the business.

What complicates matters in the entertainment industry is

that some roles hinge on maintaining a *certain* body type, sometimes in spite of what the talent wants. There are television actors that are expected to remain overweight for the sake of their characters or certain film roles that require severe weight loss in a short period of time. This industry can be physically demanding and, at the same time, prone to typecasting.

Despite this expectation, weight fluctuations are often not tolerated well in the entertainment world. I had a friend who developed an eating disorder because she perceived a pressure to remain thin while working in the business. It could have been a snide comment from someone else, or perhaps some deep-rooted self-esteem struggles. Regardless, perception often does not equal reality. I had to sit my friend down and show her the photos in my portfolio to make the point that my weight has fluctuated over the years, and I worked the entire time—the only thing that changed was what I entered on the size card prior to auditions. Our obsession with maintaining our physical ideals needs to be replaced by a focus on our unique attributes beyond just what we look like at a single moment in time.

MINDFULNESS

Whether or not you align with a particular religion, a spiritual practice is one that can help to keep negative thoughts at bay. A strong spiritual practice is one that should help you feel connected to yourself, your environment, and the people around you.

I mentioned how I like to take long walks—I cannot recommend this practice enough. Some people call it a walking meditation. I use my walking time to practice staying in the moment and enjoying nature. I also use this time to reflect on life. I some-times get into deep thought about decisions I'm facing. Every so often, I use my walking time to call up an old friend. It's okay to let your thoughts meander, but practice intentional thought, rather than noisy self-doubting thought. In fact, make it a habit to be intentional in every aspect of your life and career.

When you meet someone, regardless of who they are, look them in the eye and really listen to what they are saying. In L.A., a lot of people will shake your hand and simultaneously look over your shoulder if you're not important enough. This lack of self-awareness is the kind of behavior that will be det-rimental to your growth and won't do much to win you real friends. Don't be like that. Practice kindness and awareness to-ward yourself and others.

In the industry, with so many attractive and outgoing people in the mix, it's easy to slip into an endless party routine. And while I do recommend socializing and networking, make sure these practices don't interfere with your sleep and your health. Socializing can escalate to becoming toxic—both literally and figuratively. There are wrong-crowd types who will try to take you down with them.

You'll typically be able to suss these types out: it won't feel good to be around them, so make sure to avoid them in favor of spending time with like-minded people who have your best in-terests at heart. Use your instincts here. This goes for professional interactions, too. Especially in L.A., New York, and even Chica-go, there are people in the industry who drink and use drugs in excess. If they even hint that your success is contingent on living their kind of lifestyle, don't fall for it. It's a trap meant to get you caught in a vicious cycle. If it's not serving your mind and body, it's doing nothing good for you or your business.

SELF-RESPECT

Back in 1998, I had been living in L.A. for six months when I booked a featured extra role in a big star-studded movie. I worked on set for a month, so I had time to get to know a lot of people. Among them are a few people I still consider my friends. Unfortunately, I do not look back on this project fondly. One day, as we were filming on set, a male boom operator who had been standing nearby fixed his gaze on me for longer than what I'd consider socially acceptable. He then proceeded to make lewd comments about my body. His words were so degrading that I thought I had misheard him. He repeated his remarks—and not only had I heard him correctly, but my co-workers also heard him, too. The boom operator just didn't care who was around to hear.

By this point in my career, I had previously experienced similar gestures, but I had never spoken up. This time, I reported him to the union that was meant to represent all of us. Not only did they do nothing about it, but they also informed the powers-that-be on set about my feedback; a few days later one of the lead stars of the film gathered the entire cast and crew together for an "announcement." He spoke into the microphone that a certain cast member (me) had blown a harmless encounter out of proportion—that this particular cast member had taken some innocuous comments too seriously. He knew that everybody on set knew what had happened, who had made the allegation, and how it had been reported, and used the opportunity to issue a threat. He all but stated that we'd better keep our heads down and avoid interfering in their ingrained system of doing and saying whatever the hell they wanted without consequence, or else...

My hope is that these types of incidents are no longer tolerated. We have watched the highly publicized #MeToo trials and read the articles of individuals in positions of power taking advantage of impressionable men and women. Thanks to the bravery of the victims and whistleblowers, there are more likely to be consequences for sexual harassment today than what I faced. These days, studios spell out the consequences ahead of time. Agencies are even educating their talent on measures to take when there is an incident of sexual harassment or assault on set.

That's not to say that harassment doesn't still happen. You may encounter people, especially if you are young and early in your career, who appear very friendly and eager to help you. They may appear to you in the form of a photographer, or a producer, or an agent, making some offer of assistance or an introduction. You don't have to discredit them right away—but proceed with caution and ask questions. Do they want to meet during business hours or at night? At an office or a bar? Are they being intimidating? Does the situation feel off?

For instance, why are they so interested in your career? If they haven't seen your work before, or know next to nothing about you, it's a red flag. And if their offer seems too good to be true, it probably is. If you're on the fence, bring a friend or parent to the meeting. Research the person and learn more about their legitimacy. Someone may present themselves as a friend or advocate, and have all the right credentials, but proposition you later. If they threaten to derail your career unless you give them what they want, run. Remove yourself from the situation. Speak up—and speak loudly. These are the kind of people who ruin the credibility of the business and should lose their privileges.

There are no shortcuts to success. Build your business by the book, not by making shady backroom deals. It will feel far more triumphant when you can look in the mirror and know that you kept your integrity intact.

BEAUTY

I'm not referring to maintaining a narrowly defined "conventional beauty'—everyone can and should shine. Even if you are an unconventionally beautiful person who thinks the below advice doesn't apply to you, it does.

When you live your life on camera, certain aspects of personal maintenance require extra attention. Today's cameras are so high definition that they will capture every speck of dirt under your nails and every clogged pore: so keep that skin hydrated and fresh. Drink plenty of water throughout the day. It can be easy when you are on a job to get sidetracked and forget to drink water; it helps to carry a water bottle with you at all times. I mentioned before that you'll want your hair to look as natural as possible, but you can certainly take care of it by doing a deep conditioning mask every so often and keeping the ends professionally trimmed. Make sure to get in a good sweat, too: it will not only be great for your fitness, but also for your skin.

Keep the nails on your hands and feet clean and tidy—a good manicure won't hurt. Take your makeup off every single night and cleanse. Everyone can benefit from exfoliation and moisturization. And you don't have to spend big to look good. The best tip I received from a dermatologist: wet some baking soda with your cleanser, and there's your exfoliating scrub. I take my routine a step further and apply a face mask once a week—it's twenty minutes out of my day, and I use the practice as an unwinding activity that is also doing my skin a lot of good.

Indulging in a skincare routine can do wonders for your well-being. It's a little gift to yourself, especially when you've been working hard. Treat yo-self.

MONEY

Most business owners can attest—the first few years are tough. Expenses pile up, and your business is still relatively unknown, so people aren't rushing to buy your goods or services. You don't have much experience, and your marketing budget is in the single digits. I have a friend who is a very successful business owner. Her business did not turn a profit until year four—she is now in year 11 and killing it. She and her team lived on peanut butter and jelly with several roommates in cramped quarters, until they started generating buzz and making better business decisions.

Showbiz is not entirely different, as it requires an entrepreneurial mindset. Everyone's financial situation is different, but it can't hurt to build contingencies. Preparation is everything. Figure out your initial expenses related to photos, equipment for self-tapes and reels, commuting costs, and other incidental expenses and determine how you'll make it work. My approach was to be super mindful of my expenses, but I understand that, in today's landscape, the cost of living is more expensive than ever and cutting down on spending may not be enough. As I mentioned, I have a lot of friends who take on side hustles between jobs. If you choose to do the same, remember that auditions usually take place during business hours and casting notices typically appear the day before an audition.

When I was starting out and booking jobs sporadically, I set aside just enough money for an unexpected situation. You never know when you'll need a little extra for medical expenses—or say, if a pandemic hits and you are unable to work. Life throws all kinds of curveballs, and it's generally smart to build an emergency reserve.

In our current era, there are numerous opportunities to generate an income online. There are also temp jobs, nanny positions, construction projects, nighttime security, hospitality jobs, rideshare gigs, and more. Additionally, you might find a part-time position adjacent to the entertainment industry, like working at agencies or production companies. It is certainly possible to find a source of income that will allow you enough flexibility to audition regularly.

There are also actors and models who actively book jobs in the entertainment industry, but the minute they receive a paycheck, they spend it all on luxury goods or other non-essential items. I know it's not always sexy to be thrifty, especially in New York or L.A., but I cannot stress enough how important it is to run a tight ship with your finances. Please don't go into debt trying to keep up with the Joneses. It's just not worth it, and it will hurt your business in the long run.

When you do start to make money from your industry work, it's important to track *every single dollar* you earn. I was once signed with a fit model agency and consistently booked jobs through them—at one point, I was one of their highest-grossing models. As I mentioned in the agents' chapter, agencies receive payment from the client, then remit to you the post-split amount. I tracked the payout amounts for each job, accounting for the agency split. When tax season came and I compiled the amounts for my accountant, I noticed a glaring discrepancy in the amounts. My estimated earnings were *way* larger than what I had received from the agency. It didn't take me long to discover that there was one bad agent who had been siphoning money from each of my checks.

When the money is flowing in, it can be tempting to let your team take over your finances so you can focus all your time on expanding your career, but you must be the one in charge of your money. Even if you trust your people fully, you must track every single amount coming in and going out. Never be afraid to advocate for yourself if you see an imbalance on your ledger or bank statement. I confronted this agent, who tried to backpedal and deny any wrongdoing; he ultimately cut me a check for the full amount I was owed.

Money doesn't always flow so easily in the industry. I won't sugarcoat it: this business requires a strong stomach for volatility. If you are someone who requires a steady income stream, you may need to build extra contingencies. I've experienced months without any pay at all, and I've also had times when my mailbox was filled with residual checks (I'm not joking. It took a full day to sort through them).

Your audition breakdowns will always include the terms of payment and the rate. These rates vary to such a wild degree that it would be silly for me to give you any kind of range. You can be featured in a print ad today and earn a $200 flat fee, and the following day be booked for an **infomercial** that pays $8,000 plus $4,000 every quarter for as long as it airs. You can book a guest spot in a single TV episode today and, ten years from now, still receive residuals. I've received residual checks for a penny and for $5,000. Just as the industry culture is subject to the macro shifts in the world, so too is the pay. Certain pay rates today aren't as high as they used to be when I started, but we didn't have a plethora of streaming networks back then, either. The prominence of social media and digital advertising has also caused a lot of disruption. Brands are making more digital content, and oftentimes they will bypass hiring talent and use **stock photos** and graphics that are more suitable for a digital format.

Many companies are shifting their advertising to take a real-life storytelling approach using influencers and real people. "Real people" castings now exist: instead of drawing from a pool of entertainment professionals, casting directors will seek individuals in certain niche professions, usually by identifying them via social media. The other day I saw an ad for dog food that featured a legitimate veterinarian. As a result, having a niche is more important today than ever. Think of the many, many food shows out there, for example. If you happen to be a chef *and* an entertainment professional, you automatically have a pathway to that specific set of opportunities.

This is why you can work your whole life in a different career and still shift into the entertainment industry. Depending on your field of expertise, that first career could become a huge competitive advantage. And for the rest of you, I'm not sounding the alarm here—I'm giving you an edge over the competition. And there's a lot of it, believe me. Just being aware of the volatility in pay and the competitive landscape will prepare you early, rather than shock you later. You should also talk about your compensation expectations with your agent(s) after you've added a few jobs to your résumé and portfolio.

My advice: always keep your finger on the pulse. Find out where the money-making opportunities are, just like in any business, and think of how you'll go after them.

There's talent that you've never heard of making a good living in this business. They appear in print ads, commercials, infomercials and Broadway shows. There are people who have built their businesses doing stunt work and stand-in work. Stand-ins are part of the cast, and they play the part of a body double for the lead actor. They are an integral part of the staging process and lighting configuration. When it's time to shoot, the lead actor takes their place on set. I did body double work for the *Charlie's Angels* movie production. They had me do jumps, action poses, and power poses that would be featured in a poster.

Sure, my face would never be visible to anyone, but it was a great booking that paid well, and I had a blast on the job! Thanks to gigs like these, I never had to find a side hustle in a different industry. Instead, I immersed myself in the wide world of entertainment and made a good living by working a combination of various jobs across many different formats—and made sure not to get caught up in any one particular identity. Nowadays, I am choosy about the jobs I go after; but for thirty years, no job was too small.

When you do find yourself building your business and making a good living, think about investing in yourself. You can start paying for services to upgrade your business: for example, hire a video editor to update your reel. You can also get savvy and start trading skills with other professionals in your industry. If a photographer needs to update their portfolio, and you need to update yours, there's an opportunity for a beneficial trade.

And remember to reward yourself! Sometimes if I've worked especially hard on a project, I treat myself to a nice dinner, and I select the expensive wine. Other people I know reward themselves with a pair of designer shoes. It's important to celebrate your success and remember the things that bring you joy—but do so in moderation.

CHECKPOINT:

- Establish a health and skincare regimen.
- Practice kindness and mindfulness for yourself and others.
- Build a budget and financial plan.

SEVEN

ON THE JOB

Y ou've booked the job, now what? Take a moment and celebrate. It's an exciting event in your career: validation of all
your hard work. For me, this marks the start of something
new: new friends, new environment, new set. Up until this point,
you've done the job of portfolio-building and auditions. You've
hopefully managed to drown out the noise. You've been working
this whole time, and, until now, you've been working with the
usual crowd—your agent and your team of photographers and
beauty professionals. Now your world will open to a whole new
set of people. You'll be with other talent, with directors, producers,
the camera crew, the lighting crew, the wardrobe department, the
client, and the list goes on.

A new job can be overwhelming. If you're not the best at remembering names and faces, try as best as you can to improve.
This simple skill will be crucial. I like to associate a name with
something unique about the person. Jack with the funky glasses
is the set director. Jill, the makeup artist, mentioned her twin
Yorkshire terriers. I mentioned earlier the importance of being
kind—be mindful that this can easily devolve into too much
chumminess, where you feel like you must gossip or be unpro-
fessional in order to bond. Don't do it. Maintain your professionalism and never put anyone down, even if someone else
brings it up first. This has happened so many times in my career,

and I wasn't kidding when I said arrogant and superficial types are a dime a dozen. Just change the subject, or "take a call." Save the drama for the stage.

When you've booked a job, your agent will call you with the good news. Next, you'll receive a barrage of communication from the production crew. Usually, you'll be told to arrive with **clean hair** (no product) and a **clean face** (no makeup). Keep in mind, you'll still be in front of a lot of people, so you'll want to be comfortable but still presentable. Occasionally, typically for smaller productions, you will be asked to arrive **camera-ready**. This means you'll bring your own wardrobe and have your hair and makeup done ahead of time. Just go with what they tell you.

You will receive details down to parking information. You'll receive a **call time**: the time you are to be on set and checked in. If you receive lines, have them memorized. Practice and rehearse at home. I cannot stress enough the importance of being prepared and punctual. Productions are well-oiled machines: you are now a component of this machine, so do your part. You may hear the term **get on your mark**. They will place tape to mark where you need to stand, then the crew will test lighting and camera angles.

Pay attention to all of this, because these are the types of experiences that will only serve to make you a better professional. Having acting chops and a good screen presence is just one part of being a professional in this business. Respect all the jobs around you; notice what they are all doing. This is *your* business after all, so learn the inner workings. This will also help you to get out of your head and into the present moment. When you are fully engaged with everything that is happening on set, you'll be better equipped to perform in the environment you've been given.

When I was starting out, no one told me about all the downtime on set. I recommend bringing a book or using this time to go over your lines, if you have a speaking role. This is also a good time to meet your team, your castmates, the crew, and others on set. Get to know them, make connections. The industry can be a lonely place, but it shouldn't be. I've learned so much from the cast and crew mates.

When I look back at my career, I'm thankful for the friendships I've made along the way. There are certain people who will become lifelong friends on-the-job. Among my own "lifers" are camera people, actors, models, stylists, and more. These are important people in my life, and I never would have met them if I took myself too seriously or made a point to keep to myself. There will be a time and a place to be social on set. There are other times when you will be required to keep to yourself and stay quiet while other people do their jobs. The important lesson here is to be respectful—but when the opportunity arises, get to know the people you are working with.

ON THE JOB MEANS ON THIS JOB

When you are booked, expect to put all your other auditions on hold. Being on a set or a shoot is a full-time endeavor. If you are expected to be on set, you won't be able to pursue other opportunities. You can be on a job for a day (modeling and commercials) to several weeks and months (television and film). Sometimes a weeklong job turns into a regular job: this is a good thing. When I had a series regular job, the set schedule took precedence over other opportunities, but there were the occasional times I was able to take a job in between or go for an audition.

The best scenarios are when your longer-term jobs open future opportunities, which becomes more likely the more engaged you are with your current job. The more you work, and the more people get to know you, the more momentum you build. Just like in any client-driven business, show business is a relationship business. Your friend on the production side may refer you to a friend who is working on another project. And that brings me to my next point: **the work doesn't stop when the camera stops rolling**.

When I booked a job as a model on *Deal or No Deal*, I was excited. Initially, I wasn't sure how long I'd be working on set. I assumed it would be a few days of filming. The show became a big hit, and for the first time I was offered a regular position... and I was elated. Do what you love, and you never work a day in your life—a phrase I heard often, but never knew the true meaning until working on *Deal or No Deal*. I always loved game shows, but the excitement of working on one is something special. It was a perfect fit. I'm always playing host to friends; I love high-energy environments with big crowds, and I thrive any time I'm meeting new people from different backgrounds.

I would also have fun during commercial breaks. Some of the models took breaks backstage because it was exhausting and painful to stand for hours in heels. However, I knew that the minute I sat down, I'd never want to get back up. During commercial breaks, our warm-up guy would keep the adrenaline high by pumping the music and hyping the audience members out of their seats to dance. So instead of breaking backstage, I'd join in the fun. I interacted with the audience, helping to keep the energy flowing. I joked around with the camera crew and my fellow models on stage. I was genuinely enjoying myself. And as it would turn out, other people took notice. After a successful run, *Deal or No Deal* later transitioned to a daytime syndicated version. The powers-that-be selected two models from the original twenty-six. I was lucky to be one of them. And while I will never know for certain why I was selected—keep in mind that I worked with very talented models—I believe my off-camera attitude played a part.

I've mentioned momentum a lot. In a way, by recognizing that your work doesn't stop when the camera stops rolling, you are keeping your own momentum. That means using your off-camera time to network, being a positive presence on the crew, and avoiding gossip and undermining. Your off-camera self may be different from the person you are portraying on camera, but the same rules of any business apply in this one: people will hire you and refer you to others if you are mature, self-possessed, hardworking, and pleasant to work with.

CHECKPOINT:

- Practice remembering names and faces.
- If you are actively working on a job, even a small job or non-entertainment job, notice how you interact with others.
- Reflect on a time someone noticed your efforts, even when you didn't think they were watching.

EIGHT

NETWORKING

Remember, way back in the chapter about agents, I mentioned that every introduction could be a future opportunity. In the early days of my career, I went on a search for a hosting-specific agent. I was able to schedule a meeting with someone at a highly reputable agency known to be the hub for hosting roles. This agent had seen my résumé and reel ahead of time, so the meeting was for him to determine if I'd be a good fit for their department.

The general tone of the meeting was formal; we mostly discussed my work, but in these types of getting-to-know-you meetings, there are still two people making a connection. He had read on my résumé that I am fluent in Greek, and, because he has a person in his life who is also Greek, we connected on this shared link. I took that opportunity to be personable and let the conversation steer away from just business. He ultimately decided not to move forward with me, I thanked him for his time, and we both moved on.

Many years after that meeting, I received a call from an agent I had never met before, at an agency I had never worked with. Apparently, the original agent who passed on me all those years ago had told one of his new colleagues about me. His colleague had been looking for a host to book for a big infomercial opportunity for a Greek brand expanding their product line in the

U.S. That one meeting, years and years ago, led to a really big job. This happened for two reasons: First, I had something on my résumé that stood out from the crowd and second, I used the Greek conversation piece as an opportunity to talk about something important to me that has nothing to do with my work.

That initial meeting was a failure *on paper*. The hosting agent who I wanted to sign with rejected me. But the meeting itself was a success, as it eventually resulted in a major booking. You never know where and when an opportunity is lurking. Keep taking those meetings, highlight the facts that are unique to you, and rinse and repeat. It may not mean instant gratification, but every introduction does matter. By the way, that original agent signed me after all, ten years after our first meeting. Talk about a full circle!

KEEPING IN TOUCH

Call me old-fashioned, but I'm a fan of the handwritten card. One great way to stand out in this digitally dominated world is to send a handwritten note. I like to send thank-you cards to friends, and I also often send them to agents and casting directors after I've been booked for a job. It's a classy move, and it may ensure you are remembered.

You can order postcards with your agent's information and a headshot photo. Send these cards to casting directors when you have an upcoming theater show or spot in a commercial. If you are seeking new representation, you can send the postcards to agencies with just your personal info. You'll want to write something like "come see my play" or "check out my new commercial campaign for xyz." You'll be able to find their contact information on the casting sites that we mentioned before.

It's not a common practice these days—then again, that could work in your favor. A personal handwritten note may seem like unnecessary snail mail, but it may just go the distance for you.

NETWORKING CULTURE

Each city will have its own unspoken rules about networking. When I was working in New York, there was a culture of diving right into a relationship, whether it was with an agent or casting director. New Yorkers are the hustlers, remember? They were interested in submitting quickly and efficiently, getting the auditions, and then booking the casting. In L.A, they hustle in a different way. Theirs is more of a getting-to-know-you culture. It usually takes more time, and more meetings, before the agents and casting directors decide if you are bookable. In my experience, this process resulted in fewer auditions than what I was used to in New York.

In New York, there was a period when I was overloaded with auditions because they were constantly coming my way. I thought, if I could make it there, I could make it anywhere. It came as a shock when I was new to L.A. and the auditions came to a screeching halt. By the time I got there, I had been working in the industry for a long time, but I still had to start from scratch. In L.A., networking—and learning how to network—is imperative. It can be a long and slow process, but once you find your rhythm and your network, you'll start to get on more radars and see the results.

One final note about the cultural differences between New York and L.A. —and please keep in mind that these observations are solely based on my personal experience. In New York, you could book an extra/background role one day and be booked for a principal role the following day. There were no real structures in place, if you fit the bill and were willing to work. In L.A., there is more of a hierarchical structure where, if you're new, you are expected to work the jobs no one wants and earn your credits.

L.A. requires extra check-ins with yourself: are you comfortable with the work you are doing? You want to be taking those small jobs when you can but stay focused on leveling up and broadening your portfolio. Thick skin and a strong mindset will be assets in your early years in L.A., but that doesn't mean you have to accept any demeaning or inappropriate behavior. The problem with an ingrained culture is that many are subconsciously perpetuating it. If a person in a position of power experienced this same type of treatment early in their career, they may be inclined to repeat the cycle with the new entrants. For those of you working or thinking of working in L.A., simply being aware of this could help you in your networking endeavors and will hopefully help you keep your resolve. We have all been there at some point.

REJECTION CAN BE NETWORKING

Often, those decision-makers who rejected you in the past will call on you after you've established some clout. I've been rejected by an agent only to be contacted by that same person, after I had worked on a hit show. But those decision-makers who reject you and later call on you only know you because they've met you before. Meetings matter, even if you don't get the initial outcome you want, because they provide a reference point for you. *So-and-so from that hit show* is not the same as *so-and-so from that hit show whom I've actually met before and is really cool.*

It's no big secret that I believe in the power of momentum. The more you work, the more you *will* work. Don't take this to mean that you are likely to be booked just because you have some work under your belt. Rejection does not stop just because you have experience—but it does mean that you are likely to be exposed to more opportunities.

The moment you start heating up—when you start getting all those meetings, and all those people want to introduce you to their powerful friends—is not the time to let your guard down. This is the time, instead, to stay humble, turn up the charm, and sharpen your skills even further. Stay grounded and work even harder than before. I've seen a lot of talented people let their early successes derail them: they may take it for granted and stop improving, start looking for instantaneous results and forget that every introduction counts, try to put others down instead of giving back and building them up, or stop going to auditions altogether.

AND NETWORKING CAN BE REJECTION, TOO

When I lived in New York, I met a lot of Wall Street people. When they asked, "what do you do?", I replied that I modeled. They either thought I was full of myself for saying I am a model or that I must have modeled as a hobby—that it couldn't possibly count as a career choice. In L.A., whenever I introduced myself as a model, I felt belittled in a different way. If the people I met had been actively working in the business, whether as an executive or talent on a show, they usually followed up with "which restaurant do you work in?"

If I had a dollar for every industry person who ever belittled me, I wouldn't need to be in business. I've also encountered rude people who I met again years later and were as sweet as pie. In the entertainment business, as in life, there are good guys and bad guys, which usually means that there are people having good days and people having bad days. You never really know what's going on with someone. If you experience negative interactions, move onto the next conversation. Just remember—you are there to network, so don't waste your time with anyone who tries to deter you.

BEGINNER'S GUIDE TO NETWORKING

I imagine many of you are just starting out and may be wondering where or how to start networking. Depending on where you live, networking opportunities can vary—in L.A., they can take place at the local coffee shop. But for most places, networking typically happens anywhere there is some kind of stage. You can start networking at your acting workshops. Hang out with the theater crowd and get to know the cast and crew. There are also formal **networking events** you can sign up for.

You can even create networking opportunities yourself. Once I had established some contacts in the business, I would host networking parties for people to get to know each other. The parties were a fun way for us to unwind and connect outside of a job—but they also created synergies. My friends all worked on different projects at the time, but sure enough, there were collaborations that naturally came to fruition because they had met at one of my parties. My advice is to get yourself invited to a similar event—or, if you have made some friends in the business, host your own event. Even those of you who are in the small-jobs phase, don't overlook the opportunity to network with your cast and crew. Get into the habit early, so that you can build your network over time. And who knows—you may find your own lifers along the way.

I am a natural connector, but I understand that many people are not. Not everyone in this business is extroverted, and there is a place for the shy types among you. Being more introverted certainly does not mean you will falter in your networking endeavors—the most important thing is to be authentic and inquisitive. Seek out more one-on-one conversations. Use networking to practice being in environments with a lot of people, like a set. Bring a friend and tag-team—anything that will put you at ease in a networking environment, especially in the beginning. Regardless of whether you are extroverted or introverted, you will need to work on your conversational skills. This is a very talky business.

WORKING › NETWORKING

Networking is important. Making authentic connections, introducing yourself, introducing colleagues to friends, and bonding are necessary—and often fun—aspects of the business. But there is a thin line between networking and partying. Be careful not to get caught in a party loop, where you are slamming vodka shots on a nightly basis in the name of networking. This is a surefire way to get a party-animal reputation, and therefore to negate the whole point of professional networking.

Remember that the work doesn't stop when the camera stops rolling. That applies in pseudo-social environments where you will be around friends, yes, but also when you're around others who do not know you yet.

You may also get a whiff of FOMO every now and then. It's impossible to make all the events. The most important thing is that you are focused on working, making those auditions, and building your résumé. Networking is part of the job, but it's not *the* job—auditions are your job, being professional on set is your job, sleeping and self-care is your job. You inevitably won't be able to make every event, and if you do, you will most likely burn yourself out or teeter that line between being a networker and a partier. Balance is key here.

CHECKPOINT:

- Identify networking events in your area.
- Add professional contacts to your Rolodex (a.k.a. your iPhone contacts)
- Pay attention to how you introduce yourself to anyone you meet.

NINE

PR AND MARKETING

Think about a well-known entertainer. Now imagine all the marketing, PR, and press people who had a hand in putting their name into your head.

Social media is a free and necessary promotional tool. You should be posting as much of your work as you can on social media. Your stories can feature more of the daily-life content that will keep your followers engaged. Make sure to be consistent, and post daily if you can. If you are in the small-jobs phase and you are in a small play production, post it—but first, make sure you have permission to post. You often will not be permitted to post anything from an audition or a job. The production may also prohibit you from posting about a project until after they have promoted it according to their own PR and marketing schedule.

Anyone who comes across you in a professional capacity will look at your social media. You are your own brand, and social media is the best way to showcase it. This means that, if you haven't already, you'll need to clean up all your accounts now. Every agent, client, and casting director will ask for your social media handles and even the number of followers you have, both to ensure that you're not a liability and to get a sense of your personality and how engaging—and beloved— you are. If you have thousands and thousands of followers, that could mean instant PR for the production as well.

Your social media brand should be honest, but also project you in a good light. What is your style? What kind of workouts are you doing? Which music artists are you following? How do you do your makeup, and what do you look like without it? Just like your résumé, social media is how you tell others who you are. A thoughtful social media presence is as integral to the audition process as anything else. I've even seen people post their self-tapes.

As you build your content, be mindful of your historic posts as well. For example, if you once posted about how much you loved a particular cruise line company, and then you hear about a job for a competing brand, you'll want to go back and delete the original post. More broadly, a problematic photo or caption can become the deciding factor for a client. Try to stay away from overtly political or obscene posts and anything that has the potential to hurt your business.

Once you book a job in television or film, it may be time to hire a public relations team. Your PR team will arrange your appearances and interviews. As your career levels up, you should respond by raising your PR game. It all goes back to momentum—more jobs, more publicity, more opportunities. Often, the client or studio who hired you will have their own PR team to guide you. Your personal PR team will work to promote you by sending releases to various magazines and media outlets and setting up interviews and appearances. Media stories and profiles often feature more personal content. For example, if there is a cause you are involved with, you may be asked to talk about that. Have I mentioned that I'm Greek? Yes, I have—and sure enough, I've been interviewed for lifestyle features about Greek culture and travel.

Your appearance matters, and there are some rules of decorum regarding interviews and appearances. For example, when you are being interviewed and a host or journalist asks you a question, restate the question in your answer. For example, if they ask, "What is your name?" you should state your answer as, "Hi, my name is__" because oftentimes the question will not be heard on camera. The more of these events you attend, the more you will begin to see your photos online. The two biggest websites that contain press photos are Getty Images and Wire Image. This is the fun and glamorous side of the business. Enjoy every moment and seize the opportunity to showcase your fun side, but also keep in mind that you are representing the studio or show or film. Most importantly, you are representing yourself.

The red carpet is also called **step and repeat**. You'll walk, stop, pose, and repeat. This is to give every media outlet an opportunity to capture your photo and interview. Remember, at every corner of this business is another business. Press photos and junkets are a business, with a different set of professionals exposed to you for the first time. The press is going to help get your name and face out to the public. Just like being on set, keep your press interactions professional and friendly. You and the press are both there to do a job. At these press events, the camera is *always* rolling and there are no edits, so professionalism here can be just as important as presenting yourself on a job.

When I was starting out, I only thought about the work—I didn't consider this world of red-carpet appearances and events. The idea seemed so foreign and distant to me at the time. The more I worked, the more I became exposed to all of it. There have been glitzy, star-studded events, travel opportunities, backstage passes at rock concerts, and amazing professional opportunities. I've been able to pitch shows to networks, collaborate with brands on new products, and expand my business in ways I never thought were possible.

Thinking back to when I was starting out until now, it's like I stood in front of this giant closed door that I was able to open an inch at a time over the years, until one day it flung open, and I entered this great big world that I had no idea existed. I cannot tell you how long it will take for you to see what's on the other side of your door, and I can't tell you what to do when you get there—or how many other doors there will be, leading to other unknown places. That's the adventure you'll get to have all on your own.

CHECKPOINT:

- Get yourself PR-ready by "cleaning" your social media accounts.
- Hone your press interview skills.

I've given you a backstage pass to this industry and as many trade secrets as I could think to include—even so, your experience will be unique. It may share all the same humdrum technical details we discussed, but it will tell a different story, and feature different people in new scenarios.

Please use this book as a resource that you can revisit whenever there may be some confusion over a process or term, or anytime you need a dose of encouragement. Don't get overwhelmed, and don't give up. The more you experience the actual process yourself, the more comfortable and confident you will feel.

I realize that there are a few of you out there who might benefit from having a mentor or coach. If you've ever had a sports coach, you know that their job is to help you break bad habits and focus on your own development. I offer one-on-one consultations designed to help connect you with agents, expand your exposure and reach, and offer general career advice.

Please visit www.PatriciaKara.com to say hi and let me know what you thought of the book. I'd love to hear from you.

ACKNOWLEDGEMENTS

This book would not have been possible without the help of....

My husband, Noel LaMontagne, was there with me every step of the way. The most patient man in the world! Thank you for always going above and beyond to help me in any way you can. Your love and guidance always get me through.

My childhood friend, Renee Eliah, this book could not have been done without you. I can't thank you enough. It's because of you I was able to get this book to the finish line. Are you ready for the next one?!? And a big thank you for being there for me personally too.

My sister, my hair stylist and a big supporter throughout the years, Joanna Karamouzis. Thank you for always making my hair look so good and being my biggest cheerleader! It's because of you that mom even let me get into this business.

My nephew, Alexandros Grivas, thank you for being a great listener and always helping in any way you could throughout the process!

My sister from another mister, my bestie, Despina Grammenos. Thank you for being there for me while working on the book and so much more. You helped me get through it all!

My koubara and dear friend, Elena Evangelo. Thank you for being who you are in every way! We don't compete, we complete!

Jill Binkley & Katrina Nahikian, thank you for the love and friendship of my chosen family that have been there for me throughout so much!

Ron Fair, chef, who planted the seed for this book 25 years ago.

Rod Dyer, thank you for your friendship and artistic vision over the years.

My friend and web designer, Michael Carter, thank you for your hard work and patience.

Lisa Stuart, thank you for always being a sounding board and going through this process with me!

Craig Duswalt, thank you for the inspiration, motivation, knowledge, and advice that helped along the way.

Don Staley, thank you for the guidance in your books. I referred back to your books repeatedly throughout my process— *How to Write a Book in 30 Days*, and *Fit Mind Fit Body*.

Tom Antion & Larry Guerrera, thank you for all that time helping me build what ultimately became this book.

Vasi Koufis, thank you for being there from the start and throughout the years!

Raquel Gardner, thank you for being there for me and for your invaluable expertise in entertainment.

Sofia Spentzas-Tranchitella, Chicago photographer and friend. Thank you for capturing a lot of the big moments in my life, including this book cover!

Penny Anadiotis, Tasia Apostolopoulos, Paige Anadiotis, my Chicago Greek crew, thank you for being so helpful with everything and anything needed with the shoot and more!

Josie Volpentesta, make up artist. Thank you to my childhood friend for making me look great when I need it and of course, lending me your right-hand man for the shoot.

Cade Pearlman, make up & hair. Thank you for making me look fabulous for the book cover!

Mashawn Nix, Dina Cerchione, Bellamie Blackstone, Lindsay Hovel, Rebecca Dienno. Thank you to these amazing women from the Deal team and all their support!

Carole Contes, thank you for intro to Cheryl Benton who became my publisher. Greatly appreciate it!

Cheryl Benton, thank you for your guidance throughout the publishing process. I had a good feeling about you from the start. Glad I trusted my instincts!

Deb Mellman, Sarati Callahan, Malika Miller, Summer Bellessa, Larry Kasanoff, James Rendek, Dave Sinclair, Angelo Tsarouchas, Lou Maggio, Mike Alfieri, Kostantinos Lachanas, Alex Kalognomos, Bernard Abellada, Paul Barrutia, Heather Hegeman, Anastasia Kasimios, Derek van Pelt. Thank you for being part of the process!

It's impossible for me to thank everyone that's had an effect or played a role in my career and life, but know that no matter how big or small, positive or negative, intentional or accidental, I would not be who I am without you all.

ABOUT THE AUTHOR

Patricia Kara has been working in the entertainment business for over thirty years as an actress, model, spokesperson, and television personality. She returned to primetime television joining Howie Mandel as one of the stars of the new *Deal or No Deal* on CNBC. Patricia and Howie are the only cast members to appear on all three versions of the hit show, including NBC's original *Deal or No Deal* (Primetime and Daytime editions).

She has also appeared in *America's Got Talent, Extra, Access Hollywood,* and the *Fox Movie Channel,* as well as on *People Magazine's* "100 Most Beautiful People" list. Patricia has been a guest host on HSN and was featured in Trace Adkins' music video

"Marry for Money." She also released a workout video entitled "Fast Fitness"and launched "Dish with Trish," an online food and culture production.

She has worked with and represented companies like Time-Life, AT&T, Unilever, Johnson & Johnson, Procter & Gamble, Disney, Princess Cruise Lines, and Toyota. In her instructional series "Secrets to a Successful You" and her book, *Dream On... Now Deliver*, Patricia teaches aspiring actors, hosts, and models how to navigate the entertainment industry and set the stage for career success.

#DOND

GLOSSARY

Across the board – one agency representing a talent across multiple categories.

Ad agency – an agency responsible for putting together advertisements.

Ad lib – an improvised performance style where the talent does not use a script but creates their own dialogue.

Agent – the contract negotiating representative for talent, typically charges talent 10% (union), 15-20% (non-union).

Age Range – the age that you look, within 5-10 years above or below your actual age.

Auditions – an interview for a potential job as a singer, actor, or other performer to test suitability for employment, professional training, or competition, etc., or a reading or other simplified rendering of a theatrical work, performed before a potential backer, producer, etc.

Audition ticket – the email or notification you as the talent receives from the casting team that has information pertaining to the role, wardrobe, time, place, rate, and any special instructions.

Avail – a semi-booking status used to make sure that talent is available for a project in the event they get fully contractually booked for the project.

Back to one – is an on-set command instructed cast & crew to return to their original starting positions for a new take or retake of a scene.

Beauty shot – a clean look with minimal hair and make-up done; a more natural look.

BIO – the biographical information for talent.

Blocking – the location cues and spots for talent in a given shoot or scene.

Booking – the act of being selected and contractually attached to a commercial, film, advertisement, or other type of project.

Booker/Booking agent/Talent booker – the agent responsible for booking talent on a job after an audition.

Booking out – the act of notifying your agents and/or manager that you are not available to attend castings for any period of time and for any reason.

Breakdown – the description of the role that the casting director sends to the agent.

Buy-out – a lump sum payment for a project instead of an incremental payment over time that pays talent in entirety for a commercial, film, or entertainment project.

Callbacks – a second or third audition that reduces the talent options to the preferred talent from the original and larger pool of talent.

Call sheet – a notice provided to talent and all participants of a project that includes the schedule for the day and other important details.

Call time – the time the talent is to be on set and checked in.

Camera-ready – having your hair styled and makeup completed prior to the start of a project.

Campaign – A term that refers to the collective distribution methods for an advertising project and the different means that photo, video, or other aspects of the overall project will be used.

Casting – a scheduled event that gives talent the opportunity to audition for a commercial, film, advertisement, or other type of project (often held at a casting studio).

Casting Director - the person responsible for selecting the talent of a theatrical production, motion picture, advertisement etc.

Catalogue – modeling jobs that are specifically for publications that detail a collection of items for sale, typically for mail-order companies and online retailers.

Cattle call – a casting with an extremely large number of participants.

Character role – an actor/actress that performs unusual or unique roles other than the leading role in a performance.

Class – a shorter, singular opportunity to work on a particular aspect of the profession of an actor/actress, usually 1-2 times a week for an ongoing period.

Clean face/Clean hair – arriving to set with no makeup and no product in your hair.

Cold read – when copy/script is not provided in advance of audition and is being performed for the first time by talent at the audition.

Comedian – a type of performer that seeks to make people laugh.

Commercials – an audio or video advertisement for a good or service.

Commercial Print – photograph advertisement for a good or service.

Commission – the percentage of a talent fee that is paid to their representation.

Comp card/zed cards – a small collection of the best photos that are used as a marketing tool and business card for models.

Conflict – a scheduling issue where talent is unavailable for a desired booking, or when there is a contractual issue that prevents talent from participating in mutually similar projects.

Contract – the legal document that outlines the terms, compensation, rights, and specifics related to any actor/actress working in a commercial, film, or entertainment project.

Copy/Script – the text or lines that will be performed by talent at an audition.

Credits – the acknowledgment of an individual or entity for a contribution to a commercial, film or entertainment project

Day rate – the total daily cost to pay talent to perform on a commercial, film, or entertainment project.

Dialogue – a prepared performance by two or more actors/actresses that is used to showcase skills and performance capabilities.

Direct booking – being cast/selected to perform in a commercial, film, advertisement, or other type of project without going through the casting process.

Director – the entertainment professional responsible for guiding the talent and the performance process on an entertainment project.

Drama – a type of performance that is based on or involves conflict, tension, and consequences.

Editorial – fashion work in fashion magazine, often for a lower pay scale; generates great tear sheets.

Exclusive/Non-Exclusive – the contractual obligation that talent may or may not work with specific entities, typically for a defined timeframe.

Extra – background talent appearing in a commercial, film, or entertainment project.

Fit model – models used by designers or fashion houses that have specifically needed measurements for the defined project.

Fitting – the process of being sized and selecting wardrobe, along with necessary adjustments, prior to the shoot.

General – a meeting for talent with casting director to see if right for any upcoming projects.

Go-sees – an opportunity to meet with the client for a modeling job and to show your portfolio directly.

Headshots – a photo, focusing on the head/face and upper body, that is used as a portrait of an actor/actress and often accompanied by their résumé.

Hold – when talent is tentatively held for a project to be available to be booked if needed: not an actual booking, but a temporary restriction on availability of talent.

Host – the main talent or emcee for a television show, for example a game show, reality dating show, or awards gala.

IMDb – Internet Movie Database, an online collection of entertainment industry information, and a term used to describe the online site that allows anyone to search for information about entertainment professionals and projects.

Improv – a spontaneous and often crowd-influenced performance style where the talent acts and reacts as things happen.

Indie - full length and short films created and produced by small, independent filmmakers, not typically associated with large productions.

Industry – an alternate term for the entertainment business in any form, also: showbiz, Hollywood, the biz, entertainment.

Influencers – individuals that, due to their social media popularity, can promote products or services to potential buyers.

Infomercials/Direct-Response – a type of commercial advertisement that promotes a product or service in an informative and objective way; a 30-minute commercial.

Instincts - a natural ability that helps you decide what to do or how to act without thinking.

It's a wrap – an industry term that indicates the completion of a project.

Leading role – an actor/actress that performs the primary or starring role in a performance

Lifestyle – modeling everyday type of activities

Manager – a representative that aids in the guidance of the career of talent; typically charges talent 10-20%

Mature/Classic – modeling that refers to talent of an advanced age as defined by the project.

Markets – a term that refers to the various regional locations that a project may be produced, air, or be distributed.

Method actor – a style of performance where an actor/actress transforms themselves physically/emotionally/mentally into the role they are performing.

Mother agent – the primary agent for modeling talent.

Monologue – an individual and prepared performance by an actor/actress that is used to showcase skills and performance capabilities.

Multi-listed – multiple agencies serving multiple categories of roles (e.g., hosting, acting, modeling.)

Networking – interacting with other entertainment industry professionals in various settings to gain more professional contacts and exchange industry information.

New faces – new models starting out.

Nice casual wear – the default audition attire in the entertainment industry. Unless otherwise noted, wear dressy jeans and a blouse, or dressy jeans and a button-down.

Off-book – when copy/script must be memorized to be performed at an audition.

On your mark/hitting your mark- to stand on a designated spot for a scene, often marked with tape on the floor.

Open call (agency) – some agents will hold open hours during a set timeframe to meet talent.

Open call (audition) – an audition that is open to anyone with no limits or requirements (see also: **cattle call**).

Parts model – modeling that refers to a specific anatomical part of the body like hand, face, foot, etc.

Photo Credit – clearly acknowledging the photographer.

Pitch – a term used for the summary of a commercial, film, or entertainment project that is used to gather interest in the project and sell it to a producer.

Portfolio/Book (sometimes with agency logo) – a large collection of photos and prints used to display your experience and work, often shown during auditions for models.

POV – point of view.

Principal – talent that has a primary and significant role or appearance in a commercial, film, or entertainment project.

Print – a modeling or commercial advertising job that results in still photos promoting product.

Producer – the entertainment professional responsible for putting an entertainment project together, hiring all other professionals involved in the project, obtaining funding, providing advertising and marketing, and bringing the project to completion.

Production – the entire scope of an entertainment project encompassing the personnel and physical assets associated with the project.

Project – a term used to describe whatever an entertainment professional is working on at any time, often a short job.

Publicist – a person who handles public relations and promotional activity and strategy for talent based on a fee structure.

Reality star/shows – talent primarily known for performing in productions designed to show some aspect of real life.

Red carpet – the common term for the press and photo event that leads into a movie/project premiere or entertainment event of any kind.

Reel/Demo Reel – a brief video presentation that consists of a compilation of on-camera work that markets the experience of talent.

Referral – when someone suggests a talent to an entertainment industry professional, agent, or manager for an interview.

Release – when talent is booked or on avail for a job, but is then relieved of that booking and no longer a part of the commercial, film, or entertainment project.

Release form – a document that legally relinquishes defined rights or responsibilities of an actor/actress.

Representation/Rep –someone who works on your behalf to get you auditions/work and negotiate agreements; usually refers to an agent or manager.

Request – when the client is requesting to see specific talent for a casting.

Residuals – compensation that is paid to talent for their performance in a commercial, film, or entertainment project due to the re-airing or re-showing of their performance.

Résumé – a collective career summary of performances, jobs, special skills, training, and other relevant work that specifically describes the experience of an actor/actress/host.

Screen test – typically the final part of the audition process for a TV or film job that determines if talent is the suitable selection for the project.

Script – a manuscript or document for a commercial, film, or entertainment project.

Self-Tape – a type of audition that is done by talent on their own, and in their own space, versus a traditional audition that is done at a casting studio.

Set – the location that a commercial, film, or entertainment project is being performed.

Sign-in sheet – a questionnaire at a casting that is completed to provide all required information needed that is specific to talent.

Slate – at the start of an audition, prior to performing, where talent provides specific information like name, agency, height, etc.

Spokesperson/Spokesmodel – a job for talent that involves representing a brand, service or other entity.

Stage name – professional name, not a legal name.

Stats – a different term for the physical measurements for talent.

Step and repeat – for red-carpet appearances, the process of the talent to walk, stop, pose, and repeat.

Stock Photos –general pictures that can be used for a variety of projects at any time to create ads; royalty-free.

Stylist – the person involved in designing the appearance for any part of a project, set and wardrobe.

Syndication – the sale or licensing for publication of a project on multiple outlets; after 100 episodes, a television show can be syndicated and sold to play prior episodes on multiple networks.

Table Read – reading of script out loud by cast & crew before production starts.

Talent – an actor/actress/host/model or professional performer of any kind.

Tear sheet – a photo of a modeling job published in a magazine or ad, used to showcase in your portfolio.

Test shoots – typically an unpaid photo shoot that allows a photographer and a model to try a concept and build portfolios for the photographer and model at the same time.

Trailer (physical) – the space that talent uses to dress, prepare, rest, live, etc. while on the set of a commercial, film, or entertainment project.

Trailer (project) – the brief summation of an entertainment project that is used to advertise or sell the entirety of the project after it is completed.

Treatment – a summarized presentation or description of a commercial, film, or entertainment project used to conceptualize the larger production.

TV personality – talent primarily known for performing on television.

Under 5 or 5 lines or less – a part for an actor/actress that contains five or fewer lines of dialogue.

Usage – the contractual terms of the agreement with talent that defines the duration that a performance or project may be used.

Voice-over/VO – an audio narration or performance by talent that does not physically appear in or is necessarily portrayed in the production.

Voucher – invoice signed by talent and client at the end of job.

Workshop – a more prolonged class or series of classes, usually at least a day, to work on the profession of an actor/actres